INSIGHT GUIDES

MALLORCA
StepbyStep

APA PUBLICATIONS

Part of the Langenscheidt Publishing Group

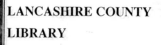

CONTENTS

Above: Mallorcan charms: Alcúdia; Andratx; Formentor; a coastal perch; the tabletop mountain of Puig de Randa

ABOUT THIS BOOK

This *Step by Step Guide* has been produced by the editors of Insight Guides, whose books have set the standard for visual travel guides since 1970. With top-quality photography and authoritative recommendations, this guidebook brings you the very best of Mallorca in a series of 14 tailor-made tours.

WALKS AND TOURS

The tours in the book provide something to suit all budgets, tastes and trip lengths. As well as covering Mallorca's capital, Palma, and the many popular coastal attractions, the routes track the mountains, plains and caves of the island's hinterland, including several lesser-known areas. The tours embrace a range of interests, so whether you are a beach baby, an art enthusiast, a foodie or wine-lover, or have children to entertain, you will find an option to suit you.

We recommend that you read the whole of a tour before setting out. This should help you to familiarise yourself with the route and enable you to plan where to stop for refreshments – options for this are shown in the 'Food and Drink' boxes, recognisable by the knife-and-fork sign, on most pages.

For our pick of the walks by theme, consult Recommended Tours For… *(see pp.6–7)*.

OVERVIEW

The tours are set in context by this introductory section, giving an overview of the island to set the scene, plus background information on food and drink, shopping, entertainment and outdoor pursuits. A succinct history timeline highlights the key events that have shaped Mallorca over the centuries.

DIRECTORY

Also supporting the tours is a Directory chapter, comprising a user-friendly, clearly organised A–Z of practical information, our pick of where to stay while you are in the city and select restaurant listings; these eateries complement the more low-key cafés and restaurants that feature within the tours and are intended to offer a wider choice for evening dining. Also included here are some nightlife listings.

The Author

Tara Stevens has been living in Barcelona for 10 years and regularly writes about Spanish lifestyle, food and wine for a wide variety of international publications. Her love affair with Mallorca began when she visited the island for the first time shortly after arriving on the mainland and was bewitched by the island's extraordinary diversity. She says: 'It certainly packs a lot into a small space. I knew about the sapphire-blue water and sand as soft as icing sugar, but who'd have guessed there would be world-class art collections, mountains to climb, local wines to discover and hip rural towns to kick back in.'

Margin Tips
Shopping tips, historical facts, handy hints and information on activities help visitors to make the most of their time in Mallorca.

Feature Boxes
Notable topics are highlighted in these special boxes.

Key Facts Box
This box gives details of the distance covered on the tour, plus an estimate of how long it should take. It also states where the route starts and finishes, and gives key travel information such as which days are best to do the route, or handy transport tips.

Route Map
Detailed cartography shows the tour clearly plotted with numbered dots. For more detailed mapping, see the pull-out map slotted inside the back cover.

Food and Drink
Recommendations of where to stop for refreshment are given in these boxes. The numbers prior to each restaurant/café name link to references in the main text. Restaurants in the Food and Drink boxes are plotted on the maps.

The € signs at the end of each entry reflect the approximate cost of a two-course meal for one, with a glass of house wine. These should be seen as a guide only. Price ranges, also quoted on the inside back flap for easy reference, are:

€€€€	60 euros and above
€€€	40–60 euros
€€	25–40 euros
€	25 euros and below

Footers
Look here for the tour name, a map reference and the main attraction on the double-page.

ART COLLECTIONS

Discover the wonders of Palma's top three art galleries (walk 2), admire the extraordinary collection at a small-town train station (tour 7), or marvel at the artistic interpretation of local wine labels (tour 14).

RECOMMENDED TOURS FOR...

FAMILY ADVENTURES

Take an alternative approach to kids' theme parks and head instead for Mallorca's extensive network of caves and grottoes (tour 11), or kick back with a bucket and spade on the longest beach in the south (tour 12).

FISHING VILLAGES

Explore the secluded bays and pint-sized fishing villages of the south (tour 12) and discover the island's best-kept secrets for local fish and seafood (tours 6 and 10).

FOODIE PARADISE

Shop for edible treasures at Palma's atmospheric delis and sweet shops (walk 3), or pack a picnic of treats from local markets (tour 13).

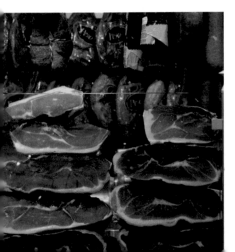

MALLORCAN ARCHITECTURE

Explore the ancient heart of Palma (walk 1), or be dazzled by the extravagant decor of Sóller's Modernista mansions (tour 7).

LITERARY GENIUS

Discover the Mallorca of George Sand and Robert Graves (tour 6), or find out how light and landscape equals poetry at the Cap de Formentor (tour 8).

HISTORICAL LEGACY

Soak up Palma's Arabic provenance, admire the Jewish quarter that helped put Palma on the map and get a taste of life at court (walk 1), admire the ancient monasteries and sanctuaries of Mallorca's hinterland (tour 13), and a bag yourself a slice of old-fashioned mountain life (tour 5).

SURF, SAND AND SUN

Escape the crowds at some of the island's most hidden beaches (tour 10), or get with the cool kids on the strands of the south (tour 12).

THE GREAT OUTDOORS

Snorkel the deserted island of Sa Dragonera off the southwest coast (tour 4) and enjoy the slowed down pace of Pollença life (tour 8).

WINE-LOVERS

Sample the island's indigenous grape varieties at the wineries of Binissallem (tour 14), or drop into some of the island's smaller vintners near Felanitx (tour 13).

OVERVIEW

An overview of Mallorca's geography, customs and culture, plus illuminating background information on food and drink, shopping, entertainment, outdoor pursuits and history.

INTRODUCTION

Often spoken of as the 'pearl of the Mediterranean', Mallorca lures with sun, sand and sea, but also has plenty of other charms to recommend it, from a cosmopolitan capital that can give most mainland towns a run for their money to a stunning interior made for active exploration.

Palma has more than enough to offer for an entertaining long weekend, but it's the 'other Mallorca', the road less travelled, that keeps people coming back for more. Whether you're looking for secluded sands or hip clubs to dance the night away in, remote country villages or soaring mountain tops, five-star golf courses or pristine diving in crystal-clear waters, the biggest of the Balearic Islands has something to suit everyone.

GEOGRAPHY AND LAYOUT

The Balearic Islands were formed nearly 100 million years ago when limestone bedrock was forced upwards, creating a peninsula jutting out to sea from the present-day Spanish coast around Valencia. Mallorca is the biggest of the four islands – Menorca, Ibiza and Formentera are the other three – and offers travellers a diverse landscape: long, sandy beaches and isolated rocky coves framed by sapphire-blue seas and backed by dramatic mountain peaks, while olive groves and vineyards fringe the sparsely inhabited interior plains. Not for nothing is the island often referred to as the Spanish mainland in miniature.

Itsy bitsy spider
Mallorca's national anthem, *La Balanguera*, is based on a children's song about a spider. The music is by Amadeu Vives – a well-known *zarzuela* composer at the start of the 20th century. It was declared the island anthem in November 1996.

Getting around

Mallorca makes for easy travelling, and the tours in this guide have been arranged to run anticlockwise around the rim of the island, starting in Palma and ending up in the centre. It is by no means exhaustive – there is still plenty to explore on your own – and hiring a car is advisable. Driving on the island is easy, and with the notable exception of the MA-15, which cuts across the centre, is generally fairly trouble-free in terms of traffic.

The main cities featured are easy to walk around, Palma included, and for tours 1, 2, 3 and 7 you can easily get around on foot or by public transport. Outside the towns there is a train network that runs from Palma to Sóller, stopping at small towns en route, and there is an extensive bus system. However, if using public transport you need to plan in advance and will need to allow extra time.

HISTORY AND ARCHITECTURE

The Romans settled in Mallorca, but had little interest in it beyond using it as a stopgap on more important mis-

sions of conquest. It was really with the arrival of the Moors in 902 that it advanced in terms of commerce and agriculture, cuisine and culture, language and education. Under the Aragonese king Jaume II the island entered a 'golden age', when some handsome little villages sprang up in rural areas such as those featured in tour 5, and heaps of money were poured into gentrifying the important towns and cities.

By the 15th and 16th centuries, however, the gap between rich and poor stoked the fire of civil unrest, which was manifested in endless uprisings, while prosperous towns like Palma, Sóller and Andratx lived in a constant state of fear of pirate attacks. Com-pounded by the arrival from mainland Europe of the plague, which wiped out a hefty chunk of the population, these were dark days indeed.

Modernista Mallorca

By the time of the Napoleonic Wars (1799–1815) many islanders had cast in their lot and moved to the New World, seduced by the promise of gold. Wealth eventually came back in the form of the lavish Modernista (Catalan Art Nouveau) mansions of the island's main towns, coloured hydraulic tiles made famous by Huguet (www.huguetmallorca.com), and the stained glass and whimsical wrought iron of the Belle Epoque. Travellers interested in architecture

shouldn't miss tours 1 and 7, which feature many of the island's finest landmark buildings.

Boom and bust

Things were quiet throughout much of the 20th century – even the Spanish Civil War (1936–9) didn't really reach Mallorca's shores – until, in 1960, the opening of Palma's Son Sant Joan airport to international traffic brought the first proper rush of tourists. This was in keeping with Franco's vision of turning great swathes of the Spanish coastline into tourist resorts along the lines of those he had heard about in Florida. Huge resorts like Magaluf and others along the east coast sprang up over the next 40 years, but the

Below: the city walls in Alcúdia

flow of foreign cash slowed, as by the 1990s the island had managed to position itself alongside the Costa del Sol and Benidorm with a reputation for dishing up a particularly virulent strain of mass tourism, that put many people off coming.

The new Mallorca

But Mallorca has never been a place to sit back and let things happen, and the early years of the 21st century have seen it smarten up its act considerably, in keeping with the needs of a more discerning traveller. Boutique hotels sprang up in Palma, and the tourist office stopped advertising sun, sea and sangria and started marketing *agroturismos* (smart rural hotels, often with a foodie focus), cycling holidays and a vast portfolio of cultural events. Even the budget airlines have come under fire from some tourism officials, who say they attract the 'wrong sort of tourist'. While that may be somewhat misplaced – it is not unheard of for millionaires to check in with easyJet, after all – 21st-century Mallorca is definitely a class act.

Climate

Mallorca's climate is temperate most of the year, although it does get its wintry spells (even, on some occasions, snow in the high Tramuntana). November, December and January can also see many businesses on the island closed. July and August, by

contrast, can get extremely hot and the hotels rammed. Generally, then, spring and autumn are the best times to visit, with balmy temperatures by day, cool evenings and fewer crowds. From January to March it can be wet, so if you're here on a hiking holiday, do come properly equipped.

Population

The population of Mallorca is just over 700,000, nearly half of whom live in Palma. Compare that to the 6 million-plus tourists the island welcomes every year and you get a sense of just how hospitable your average Mallorquín can be. A sizeable chunk of the population is made up of resident expats (mainly British, German and Scandinavian). Mallorquíns are a generally friendly bunch – especially if you take the trouble to learn a few words of Catalan – and you will find them warm, helpful and welcoming, provided you respect their culture and environment.

Local customs

Islanders, with the exception of farmers in very rural communities, are bilingual, speaking both Mallorquín (a dialect of Catalan and the first language of the island) and Castilian fluently. In the main tourist areas you will find that many people also speak some English and German, and there is nearly always someone about to help should you find yourself stuck.

Do bear in mind that Mallorcan hours follow those of Spain: shops open around 10am, lunch is served from 1.30–3.30pm and dinner from 9pm onwards. You can drop in for a tapa and a glass of wine in any bar at pretty much any time of day, but many places are closed on Sunday night and all day Monday. The main museums are generally open all day (although many close on Monday), but smaller ones may shut for a siesta. And out of season (November to the end of January) many places close down altogether – which is great if you want an extremely quiet holiday, but something to consider if you have your sights set on a certain hotel or restaurant.

Politics and economics

Something of a political conundrum, Mallorca has no fewer than 35 political parties, each of which competes for a seat in the council of 53 municipalities. The island was governed by a coalition of five different left-wing and nationalist parties, headed by the Partit Socialista de Mallorca (PSM), but in the May 2011 regional elections the right-wing Partido Popular won an undisputed overall majority.

Tourism, and the related infrastructure, is now the main source of income, accounting for around 80 percent of the island's GDP. More than half of all residents work in the sector, and people come from other parts of Spain as well to take up seasonal jobs.

Above from far left: Magaluf remains a byword for sun and sea package tourism; restaurants follow standard Spanish hours so be prepared to eat late; elaborate Belle Epoque ironwork in Llucmajor.

Rafa Nadal Tennis ace Rafael (Rafa) Nadal came from humble beginnings in the town of Manacor. He rose to fame as a teenager and is now known as one of the greatest tennis players of all time. By By 2011, he had won 10 grand slam singles tournaments, including six French Opens, and the 2008 Olympic gold medal.

FOOD AND DRINK

It took Spain a long time to realise that its larder was as well stocked and delicious as that of France, its chefs and restaurants every bit as talented. Now it has there's no stopping it, and Mallorca is no exception.

From traditional *cellers (see p.80)* and fishermen's shacks to the proponents of *Nou Cuina Mallorquina* (New Mallorcan Cuisine) – creative young chefs serving innovative food not just in Palma, but all over the island – the sheer diversity of food and eating in Mallorca is thrilling, but you do need to know where to look. The restaurants section of this guide *(see p.100)* therefore focuses on more local places to eat, and avoids fast food and the bland, 'international-style' meals on offer in the bigger resorts. More importantly, armed with just a little background knowledge of the island's rich culinary heritage you'll be well set up for seeking out hidden gems of your own.

LOCAL CUISINE

Menú del día
The lunchtime menu is an economical way to eat, as you usually get three hearty, and generally good quality courses with bread and a glass of wine for a low price (typically around €10–12).

Traditional *cuina Mallorquina* (Mallorcan cuisine) reaches its height in the old-fashioned *cellers* of the hinterland, but can be found in many other places, too. Local, humble ingredients – fruit, vegetables, pulses and grains – provide the backbone of the cooking, complemented and enhanced by locally caught fish and seafood (there are plenty of functioning fishing ports,

some with excellent restaurants, dotted around the coast, as well as in Palma). Pork – particularly the native *porc negre* – appears in various guises, and island lamb, rabbit and small game birds like partridge and quail are also excellent. Increasingly, small producers of cheese, honey, chocolate and other delicacies are also emerging.

Two ways with bread

In nearly every restaurant in Mallorca you will be offered *pa amb oli* (bread and oil), although these days it's ramped up a bit with a small dish of olives and one of *alioli* (garlicky mayonnaise). It's at its best when made with a dark, rustic island bread.

For breakfast you are more likely to be given *pa amb tomaqàet* – the ubiquitous Catalan snack of toasted bread rubbed with a juicy tomato and drizzled with olive oil and a sprinkle of salt. It sounds simple, but is one of the great treasures of the Catalan kitchen and not to be missed. Many hotels serve it as part of their breakfast buffet, while tapas bars do theirs topped with charcuterie, plump little anchovies or *escalivada* (a salad of roasted vegetables).

All power to the pig

For centuries, pork has been the cornerstone of the islanders' diet. Every family, no matter how poor, fattened a pig every year and, after the *matança* (slaughter), filled the larder with sausages, chops and lard, which formed the foundation of many dishes, both sweet and savoury.

At its most challenging, pork is presented in the form of *frit Mallorquí*, a platter of fried nasty bits liberally seasoned with fennel and mint. More easily digested, perhaps, are the succulent *sobrasadas* (soft pork sausage flavoured with *pimentón*), *butifarró* (coarse grilling sausages), *blanquet* and *camaiot* (cured pork sausages with varying degrees of fat and blood) that you see hanging from the rafters of restaurants and delicatessens.

Popular pork dishes are *llomb amb col* (pork rolled in cabbage leaves and baked) and *arròs brut* (rice with pork or sometimes chicken). *Lechona asada* (roast suckling pig) is really a Christmas dish, but may be found on menus at other times and has been indicated where relevant throughout the tours sections of this book.

A vegetarian cornucopia

Unlike in much of Spain, vegetarian foodies will do well here. The island has a rich variety of vegetables – among them aubergines, peppers, chard, crunchy lettuces, good potatoes and juicy tomatoes (including

Above from far left: *tumbet* and hams: vegetarians and carnivores will do equally well in Mallorca.

Above: pick up local produce at one of Mallorca's food markets (*see p. 16*).

Left: buy vegetables at Sineu Market, the oldest on the island (*see p.76*).

the revered *tomàtiga de Ramellet*, a vine tomato with a thick skin grown specifically for making *pa amb tomàquet*, and which you see hanging on strings in markets all over the island).

In summer, dishes such as *trempó*, a salad of tomatoes, onion and green peppers; are popular; *tumbet*, aubergines, potatoes and sweet red peppers covered in tomato sauce and beaten egg and oven-baked, is a great favourite, as are *aubergines farcides*, aubergines filled with minced meat and tomato sauce.

Soup for the soul

Sopas mallorquinas – invariably referred to in this plural form – are ubiquitous. They are soups made of seasonal vegetables and poured over *pa pagès* (country bread sliced very thin). An interesting variety is the *sopes de matances*, which include small pieces of pork and *setas* (a type of mushroom).

Fish and seafood

Although there are as many fish dishes as there are varieties of fish, two especially worth trying are *anfós al forn* (baked sea bass) and *caldereta de peix* (spiced fish stew, a version of bouillabaisse). *Caldereta de llagosta*, a a rich lobster and tomato stew laced with saffron that is a Menorcan speciality, is also popular, particularly along the north coast. Look out also for *pescado al sal* – whole fish baked in a thick shell of sea salt to preserve the flavour and juices – which, surprisingly, doesn't make the fish taste too salty. Finally, if you're a seafood-lover, don't miss the sweet, pink prawns from Sóller – wildly expensive but absolutely worth it.

Food markets

If you're into food, don't miss a trawl around Mallorca's various fresh-product markets (especially if you have opted for a self-catering holiday). Aside from the sheer bounty of produce available, it's a great way to rub shoulders with local people and immerse yourself in the true flavour of the community. Great buys include olive oil, olives, cheese and charcuterie, locally made jams and honey, and of course seasonal fruit and vegetables.

Tuesday morning: head for Artà, which has a wide range of foodstuffs as well as quality local crafts – see tour 10.

Wednesday morning: Sineu on the central plains is excellent for a taste of old village life, and is one of the very few that still has a livestock section. If you're following tour 12, the afternoon market in Colònia de Sant Jordi is an atmospheric place to end the day and pick up snacks for a casual dinner on the beach.

Thursday morning: Deià's weekly market is filled, as you might expect, with more upmarket treats and the works of local artists and craftspeople.

Friday morning: stop by to pick up local wines in Binissalem as well as tapas items to go with them. Picnic food doesn't get better.

Saturday morning: Palma has three permanent markets, but the farmers'-cum-artisan market that comes into town on Saturday is second to none.

Sunday morning: gather supplies for tour 13 in Felanitx, or for tour 6 in Valldemossa, and find yourself somewhere to have lunch with a view.

Cakes and pastries

Savoury pastries are found in bakeries *(panaderías)* or pastry shops *(pastelerías)*. *Empanades* are small round pies filled with meat and peas; *coca de verdura* is similar to a pizza but is rectangular in shape and eaten cold; while the *cocarois* is half-moon-shaped and filled with *bledes* (chard).

Dolç (desserts) range from the typical *gelat de ametla* served with *coca de gató* (almond ice cream with almond cake) to large, star-shaped biscuits called *crespells* and *coca de patata* (a sweet bread that is a speciality of Valldemossa), as well as *greixonera de brossat*, a type of cheesecake. The *ensaimada*, a spiral-shaped, sugar-dusted confection, is most commonly eaten with coffee at breakfast time.

WHERE TO EAT

At breakfast time you might stop at a pavement café for a cup of coffee and a pastry, then pop into a tapas bar or market stall mid-morning for a quick pick-me-up (a glass of cava or vermut, perhaps) and a tapa. For lunch Spanish workers head to a neighbourhood restaurant for a *menú del día* (an inexpensive set meal), then maybe have another tapa somewhere in the early evening. Dinner can be formal or consist of a *tapeo* (a tapas hop) around several bars. Naturally, the best fish restaurants are on the coast and around port areas, while the best fine dining is scattered across the island. And don't discount restaurants in the centre, which showcase some of the best traditional cooking.

DRINKS

Mallorca's wine industry goes from strength to strength, and you won't go far wrong if you stick to locally produced wines *(see tour 14, p.78)*. Cava (sparkling wine from Catalunya) is also popular, as is a *caña* (a small draught beer). Most of the beer hails from mainland Spain: San Miguel, Moritz and Estrella de Galica are all good brands to try. Neighbouring Ibiza's Isleña is a light, refreshing pilsner-style beer available all over the island.

PRACTICALITIES AND TIPPING

As in the rest of Spain, people in Mallorca eat late. Lunch is generally from 1.30pm to 3.30pm, dinner from around 9.30pm until late. Restaurants that open their their doors earlier tend to be touristy, but this can be useful if you're travelling with children.

Tipping is a bit of a grey area. If you want to round up to the nearest euro at the bar if you've only had a snack, that's fine, but not expected. Leaving 5 percent at lunch or dinner is acceptable, and if you are eating somewhere high end, leaving 10 percent is the honourable thing to do.

Above from far left: catch of the day; the Forn des Teatre is a Palma bakery that specialises in *ensaimadas*; Mallorca has a thriving wine industry.

SHOPPING

It may not be Madrid or Barcelona, but Mallorca does have a few treats for the consummate shopaholic. Eschew designer labels in favour of island arts and crafts or gourmet products and you'll find a treasure trove of purchases to be discovered.

If Palma is a hotspot for local fashion, interiors and shoes (many of the brands cheaper than they would be on the mainland), the rest of the island has fostered a high-class cottage industry of locally made goods. The discerning traveller can pick up beautiful textiles to translate into bed and table linen back home, classy handmade espadrilles (the rope-soled summer shoe traditional to Spain as a whole), some of the world's finest olive oil and almonds, and a host of other quirky trinkets for gifts.

WHAT TO BUY

Glass, pottery and ceramics

There are two glass-blowing factories that can be visited: Lafiore, at S'Esgleieta 7km (4 miles) from Vall-demossa *(see tour 6, p.44)*, and Vidriera Gordiola, just before Algaida on the Palma–Manacor road. Both do a strong line in wacky, psychedelic-coloured bowls and glasses.

The village of Pòrtol, a short distance northeast of Palma, has the most working kilns on the island. It is also the birthplace of *siurells*, the red, white and green clay-figure whistles, said to have originated in Muslim times.

Textiles

The *roba de llengües* (cloth of tongues, pronounced 'yengos'), is named for the colourful, tongue-shaped patterns stamped onto a cotton-linen weave. It's extremely popular for home textiles – tablecloths and bed linen as well as upholstery – and can look surprisingly chic and contemporary. Working looms clatter away at the Museu Martí Vicenç in Pollença *(see tour 8)*, but there's a greater selection to buy at Herederos de Vicente Juan Ribas, Carrer Sant Nicolau 10, in Palma.

Leather and straw

Mallorca used to be renowned for the quality of its leather goods, but the industry has declined considerably. Inca is still home to the better-known brands and factory outlets like Camper and Farrutx. Elsewhere you will find *abarcas*, the slipper-like sandals from Menorca that have been worn by peasants for centuries and now come in a range of colours for around €25. They've become something of a cult item in recent years, the hipster alternative to the espadrille.

In Palma, the old-fashioned Cesteria el Centro makes straw baskets, sunhats and espadrilles; Alpargateria

The rebaixes
Sales in Spain are fantastic, not least because they seem to get longer and longer each year. You'll get the cream of the crop at the start, but the real bargains towards the end. Winter sales start on 7 January and last until 6 March; summer sales last all July and August.

Llinás, Carrer Sant Miquel 43, also sells traditional espadrilles and funky straw shopping bags.

Food and drink

Ensaimadas (see p.17) are sold in individual or family sizes, in appropriate packages for export. Buy them in just about any bakery in Palma or in the departure lounge at the airport. Markets are the best places for olives, cheese and charcuterie, or go to an old-fashioned deli like little Colmado Santo Domingo *(see tour 3)*. Vineyards are found around Binissalem–Consell–Santa Maria *(see tour 14)*, and in the southeast around Felanitx, and wines are worth buying here. Mallorca is also known for its herbal liqueurs, the most popular being the aperitif Palo Tunel, made in Bunyola.

Antiques and flea markets

There are various well-known antiques shops, most notably in Santa María, Pollença and Sóller. In Palma, Antigüedades Casa Delmonte, La Rambla (Via Roma) 8, and Midge Dalton at Plaça Mercat 20, are good but expensive, while the Baratillo (flea market), which takes over the Avinguda Gabriel Alomari Villalonga every Saturday morning, is great for bargains. Go early.

Palma's stores

Avinguda Jaime III is lined with designer and high-street stores selling fashions, jewellery and gifts. El Corte Inglés, Spain's biggest department store chain, is a good one-stop shop for national and international brands. The Passeig del Born has an interesting variety of shops, ranging from high-quality leather luggage and accessories at Loewe to the city's flagship Zara.

Librería Ereso, one of the best bookshops in the city, is in Carrer Paraires, near Plaça Rei Joan Carles I, and there are a number of small fashion boutiques on nearby Carrer Verí.

Above from far left: Mallorca's shopping specialities include locally-blown glassware, straw baskets and ceramics.

Opening hours
Most small shops open from 10am–2pm and 5–8pm. High-street chains and department stores generally open all day, often until 10pm. With the exception of very touristy areas, most shops shut on Sunday. If you are self-catering, be sure to stock up.

Left: Plaça Mayor hosts markets several days of the week.

ENTERTAINMENT

Mallorca is as lively and highly cultured as one could hope for in a place of its size. To quote the great Catalan artist Santiago Rusiñol, islanders 'take the moon' as others 'take the sun', so come prepared to spend long, balmy nights beneath the stars.

The most popular of all Spanish pastimes is to sit out on a plaza in the cool of the night, sipping cold *cañas* (small draught beers) and chatting the night away. Even the smallest of villages seem to burst into life the minute the sun goes down, but Mallorquíns, like all Catalans, are also great patrons of the arts, and Palma is blessed in having a city council that throws considerable funds at keeping her citizens happy. Note that much of the performance art is in Catalan or Spanish, which makes it tough going for non-speakers, though there's plenty else to enjoy that doesn't depend on knowing the language.

THEATRE AND FILM

Theatrical performances and classical concerts usually start at 10pm, and can be found at the fabulously renovated Teatro Principal and the Teatro Municipal (theatrical performances, of course, will be in Spanish or Catalan), and the Auditorium *(see p.106)* – home to the Ciutat de Palma Symphony Orchestra. There is one original-language cinema – Multicines Renoir, Carrer Emperatrix Eugenia 6 – which has occasional midnight screenings.

All the island's a stage
In July and August it seems that life in Mallorca becomes one long concert, especially in the towns of Deià, Pollença, Valldemossa and Artà, which stage world-class classical music festivals.

DANCE

Classical or contemporary dance performances are few and far between, but there are a couple of decent salsa and samba bars, including Made in Brasil *(see p.106)*, which also offers dance classes. Flamenco isn't big in Mallorca as it has little to do with the island culture, but you can sometimes catch performances at La Caseta Rociera on Palma's Passeig Marítim.

MUSIC

Music thrives in Palma, ranging from classical guitar competitions and jazz festivals to piano recitals. There is also a strong jazz and blues scene in the small bars of the old city. Free outdoor concerts – jazz, rock and classical – are held in the beautiful setting of the Parc de la Mar *(see walk 1, p.28)* on some summer evenings. A bar serves drinks and snacks, and there's a party atmosphere.

BARS AND CAFÉS

Bar-hopping is the favoured nocturnal pursuit in Palma, and few things beat kicking back on a terrace with a glass of wine, a beer or *café con hielo* on a balmy

Above from far left: an alfresco traditional dance performance; relaxing with a drink at a café is all part of the Spanish idyll.

summer night. Café Lírico in Plaça de la Reina or La Bóveda nearby at Carrer Boteria 3 fill up around 10pm and stay full until their doors close at 2–3am. If it's cocktails you seek, don't miss Ábaco *(see p.106)*. It's a Palma institution – kitsch, camp, exotic and expensive, and no trip is complete without it.

NIGHTLIFE

In the large resorts, notably Magaluf, clubs and discos keep going all night, catering mainly to a very young tourist crowd. The scene is less classy (and drug-fuelled) than in Ibiza, and the best way to find out what's happening is to pick up leaflets in bars in Palma and the rest of the island.

In Palma itself the scene is rather more sophisticated, attracting an older, better-heeled crowd who like their dancing after dinner, their cocktails made with premium liquor and to be in bed by 3am. There are some places where you can dance until dawn, such as the legendary Tito's on the Passeig Marítim and super-hip beach clubs like Puro Beach at Cala Estancia or Virtual Club *(for all of above, see p.107)* at Illetas, where the beautiful people go.

DINNER AND SPECTACLE

A phenomenon that arrived a few decades ago is the 'dinner and spectacle' evening, and despite the rather cheesy overtones they are immensely popular. They range from those suitable for children, such as at Pirates *(see p.107)* in Magaluf, to a rather swankier affair at the Casino *(see p.107)* up the road. Dress is smart-casual, and you will need your passport to get in.

Left: Magaluf's nightlife scene is ever-lively.

OUTDOOR PURSUITS

It's easy to think of Mallorca as a place with a great beach and little else, but the island is blessed with a diverse landscape that makes it perfect for any number of outdoor pursuits and sports activities.

Of all the Balearic Islands, Mallorca's terrain is the most rewarding, ranging from the gently undulating hills across Es Pla (the central plains), which are ideal for cyclists, to ancient stone paths that crisscross the Tramuntana. You can ramble along cliff paths leading down to secluded bays or tee off on some of the world's most stunning golf courses. Highlights are included within the tours sections, such as the walk to an ancient Trappist monastery *(see tour 4, p.39)*, or as part of the long-distance GR-221, but see below to get some idea about what else is out there.

BEACH-HOPPING

There are some 80-odd beaches on Mallorca, ranging from wild and windswept to idyllic, isolated coves, and everything in between. Beaches around the Bay of Palma are fairly busy, trendy and well catered for in terms of bars, restaurants and beach clubs. West coast beaches are less accessible and shingle rather than sand, but great if you like isolation. The north coast is mainly family-oriented, with a few hidden gems at the northeastern tip *(see tour*

10, *p.61)*. The east coast is largely built up, save for some less developed strands like that at Canyamel *(see tour 11, p.64)*, and the south, once you get away from the Bay of Palma, is wild and unspoilt and all the lovelier for it.

CLIMBING

More extreme sports are only just starting to take off, but climbing is gaining a firm foothold among more adventurous travellers, thanks to the stunning landscape. Much of it is done on already bolted-in limestone surfaces, a lot of which rise up spectacularly from the sea. Nearly all of it is in the northwest Tramuntana. For extra information, www.rocksportmallorca.com is a good resource.

CYCLING

Over the past few years Mallorca has become a massive destination for keen and professional cyclists – Tour de France training is done here, for example – particularly across the central plains. Good roads and varied terrain mean it offers something for everyone, and in 2010 the island attracted nearly 55,000

The naked truth
The Spanish are not prudish, but if you want to get your kit off you should head for designated beaches (some of the nicest on the island anyway). Recommended are Es Trenc (the central part), El Mago (signposted from the road to Cap de Cala Figuera, Bay of Palma) and Cala S'Almunia (walkable from Cala Llombards heading south).

cyclists. Organisations like Mallorca Cycling Tours (www.majorcacyclingtours.com) are a good way to go, but you could approach it at a luxurious level, for example at Hotel Reads *(see p.99)*, which offers state-of-the-art kit as well as experienced guides and trainers.

GOLF

There are 12 18-hole golf courses on Mallorca. Some of the finest, including the prestigious Son Vida, are clustered around the Bay of Palma. You can get discounted green fees through the website www.simplymallorcagolf.com, as well as bags of information on each course. Many hotels offer golfing packages, and there's a good range of places to choose from, like hip, boutique Hotel Feliz *(see p.94)*, or grand de luxe Son Net (www.sonnet.es). You can also pay day green fees at most of the courses.

HIKING

The GR-221 (or Stone Wall Way) is the most popular hiking trail on Mallorca and takes you through the entire Tramuntana (about eight days). There are five refuges to stay in en route, and www.conselldemallorca.net has excellent information, including downloadable maps and route planners. If you want to do something less strenuous, there are innumerable well-marked trails all over the island, and new and improved paths are opening all the time.

HOT-AIR BALLOONING

The most spectacular and most memorable way to see the island, riding high over the plains and mountains and deep blue sea, is not as inaccessible as you might imagine. Flights cost from €195 and include champagne. Check www.balloonflightsspain.com.

WATER SPORTS

The main activities are sailing, windsurfing and scuba-diving. Palma is a good place to charter a sailing boat if you want to go island hopping (www.charteryachtsmallorca.com). The best area for scuba-diving is the west coast, where sheer cliffs and sheltered bays attract the most diverse sea life. West Coast Divers, www.divinginmajorca.com, offers a wide selection of dives. The near-constant winds of the Cap de Ses Salines attract serious windsurfers, but learners are better off on the north coast; check www.windfriends.com.

Above from far left: Mallorca offers a wide choice of outdoor activities, from cycling and windsurfing to bird-watching and snorkelling in the crystal-clear waters.

Birdwatching

Mallorca is a great place for birdwatching. Migrant birds visit in spring, and some stay throughout the summer. As many as 200 different species have been recorded. The place where you are most likely to see a wide variety is the Parc Natural S'Albufera on the Bay of Alcúdia. The Parc Natural de Mondragó in the southeast is another good spot, especially for seabirds, and you may spot black vultures as well as other more common birds of prey in the wild Tramontana region.

HISTORY: KEY DATES

For a small island Mallorca has a lot to say for itself. Home to prehistoric man as far back as 5700BC, it's been ruled by Romans and Moors, gained and lost independence, founded missions in California, and stood up to Napoleon. Today, it's one of the most affluent islands in the Mediterranean.

EARLY PERIOD

1300–1000BC	Talayotic period.
123BC	Mallorca absorbed into the Roman Empire.
2nd century AD	Christianity established.
707	First Muslim attack.
902	Annexation to the Emirate of Córdoba.
1087–1114	Mallorca becomes an independent *taifa*.
1114	Pisan-Catalans conquer Mallorca; siege of Palma lasts eight months; after sacking the city the invaders leave.
1115–1203	The Almorávides, a tribe from North Africa, arrive to help the Mallorcan Muslims and stay on to occupy the island, which experiences a period of prosperity.

THE 13TH TO 18TH CENTURIES

1229	King Jaume I of Aragón conquers Mallorca. Work begins on Palma Cathedral.
1276	Death of Jaume I and creation of the independent Kingdom of Mallorca ruled by Jaume II.
1285	Catalunya attempts to recover the Kingdom of Mallorca by force. Later expedition returned by order of the Pope.
1324–44	Reign of Jaume III, bringing economic prosperity.
1344	Troops of Pedro IV of Aragón invade and reincorporate the islands into the Kingdom of Aragón.
1479	Kingdoms of of Castile and Aragón, including Mallorca, united. Economic decline begins.
1700	Felipe de Bourbón ascends to the throne. Beginning of the War of Spanish Succession.
1785	Treaty of Algiers signed, ending piracy while establishing the Mallorcan 'corsairs'.

The Talayots
These ancient conical structures are the remnants of prehistoric life on the island – most likely watchtowers or possibly dwellings at the centre of villages. There are several still left on the island, the best being at Capocorb Vell, on the south coast, and Hospitalet Vell on the east.

THE 19TH CENTURY

1808–13	The War of Independence against Napoleonic troops.
1820–2	Massive emigration to Algeria and South America.
1837	First steamship line between Mallorca and mainland.
1879–98	Period of prosperity thanks to wine and almond trades ends with arrival of the *phylloxera* epidemic and loss of Spain's last colonies.

20TH CENTURY TO THE PRESENT

1936–9	Spanish Civil War.
1939–75	Dictatorship of General Franco.
1960s	Mass tourism brings prosperity, but great environmental damage.
1983	Five years after the Statute of Autonomy, the Balearics become an autonomous province and Mallorquí the official language.
1986	Spain joins the European Community (now the EU).
1990s–present	The Balearics enjoy the highest per capita income in Spain.
early 21st century	The government initiates measures to encourage eco-friendly tourism and move the island's image upmarket.
2011	The Partido Popular wins a majority in the island government in May elections.

Above from far left: the 14th-century city walls of Alcúdia; an illustration in Petra shows their famous son Fray Junípero Serra *(see below)*.

Leading lights
Two of the most influential Mallorcans were philosopher and scientist Ramón Llull (1235–1315), credited with being the author of the first major work of Catalan literature, and Fray Junípero Serra (1713–84), founder of the missions in California.

Left: Ses Païsses, a Talayotic bronze age settlement.

WALKS AND TOURS

HISTORIC PALMA

This half-day tour offers a distilled version of the history of Palma. Explore the narrow lanes of the medieval Jewish quarter – now also home to chic boutiques and trendy restaurants – and add drama with a peek at the fortress-like cathedral, serene Arabic Baths and a king's secret garden.

DISTANCE approximately 3km (2 miles)

TIME Leisurely half-day

START Parc del Mar

END S'Hort del Rei (The King's Garden)

POINTS TO NOTE

This walk is ideal for first-time visitors to Palma, showcasing the oldest, prettiest part of the old city known as Sa Calatrava. Because the sights along it are open year-round, it works at any time of year and could easily connect with all or some of walk 2 (p.33), if you wanted to cram a lot into a day.

Columbus's cartographer

One of the great Jewish celebrities of the 14th century was the cartographer Jafuda Cresques, who was credited with drawing up the first Catalan Atlas as well as the maps used by Christopher Columbus. His house still stands on Carrer Botones, due east of the Church of Monte Sión, but it is not open to the public.

Palma has a colourful cultural history. Founded by the Romans in 123BC as Palmeria, it was a fairly unimportant backwater until the arrival of the Moors in AD902. Seeing the city's potential, they built mosques (one where the cathedral now stands), bathhouses and other tokens of civilised life.

This tour starts where the 21st century and the Middle Ages meet, at the Parc del Mar.

PARC DEL MAR

Start your walk at the entrance to the Moorish Walls at the western end of the **Parc del Mar ❶**, which gives the most commanding view. The contemporary concrete and wood landscaping provides a striking contrast to the old city and the sea beyond. In the middle is an artificial lake designed to reflect Palma's imposing cathedral, an essential stop for photography enthusiasts. It is also home to a number of modern sculptures, including a vibrant mural by Joan Miró.

Follow the walls around to the east and you will eventually reach a plain

Food and Drink

① CAFÉ MURADA

Paseo Dalt Murada 2; tel: 971 714 278; B, Br, L, AT; €

This hippie-chic little café is tucked into the walls of the old city at the far end. It's a great place for healthy breakfasts and a *café con leche* on the sunny terrace before you start your tour, and also does a good, light lunch if you find yourself back here later on.

arch – the **Porta de la Portella ❷** – the official doorway to the Casc Antic (Old City) under Arabic rule and the heart of the Call (Jewish quarter) during the 13th and 14th centuries (keep going if you want a coffee at the **Café Murada**, see ⑪①, before you start). Straight ahead at Carrer de la Portella 5 is the **Museu de Mallorca ❸** (tel: 971 717 540; Tue–Sat, June–Oct 10am–2pm, 5–7pm, Nov–May 9.30am–1.30pm, 4–6pm, Sun 10am–2pm; free). Housed in the resplendent mansion Ca La Gran Cristiana, it is well worth a stop to take a peek at Roman remains, Gothic and Islamic art, and get a sense of the rich history of this comparatively small city.

Palma's Jewish heart

This compact, car-free neighbourhood of narrow cobblestoned streets was home to one of the most prolific and wealthy Jewish communities in the entire Mediterranean in the Middle Ages, although Jews had been here since Roman times *(see margin tip, left)*. This cultural mix accounts in some part for the diverse architectural styles that make up one of the most handsome cities in the Mediterranean, much of which spun out from a sacred hill in the centre known as **Monte Sión ❹** – now the site of a church.

ARABIC BATHS

From the museum, turn right onto Carrer Pureza and immediately right again onto Carrer Serra and you'll find one of the last remaining vestiges of the Moorish occupation. The **Banys Arabs ❺** (Arabic Baths; Carrer Serra

Above and below: views from and around the Parc del Mar.

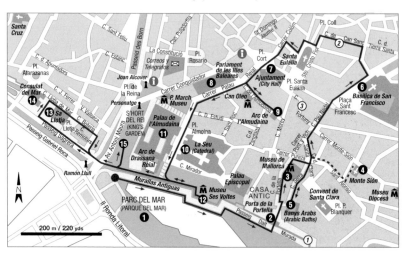

7; tel: 971 721 549; Apr–Sept daily 9.30am–8pm, Oct–Mar 9.30am–6pm; free), which once housed the hot baths, are well preserved, with a pristine cupola pinpricked with tiny skylights. The secret, shaded gardens also provide a superb retreat if you're looking for somewhere shady to escape with a book for an hour or two.

CATHOLIC CHURCHES

Head north along Carrer de Santa Clara, then right onto Carrer Pont y Vich and Carrer Pau Nadal and you'll pop out on pretty Plaça Sant Francesc, where there is a small chapel of the same name. The **Basílica de San Francisco** ❻ is something of a hidden treasure, notable for having one of the most beautiful cloisters in Spain, with delicately carved columns and arches. It is also the final resting place of Ramon Llull *(see p.25)*, who was credited with penning the first great literary work in Catalan.

Palmas's oldest café

A couple of streets away heading north, the beautifully tiled 18th-century **Can Joan de S'Aigo**, see ⑪②, on Carrer de Can Sanç 10, was Joan Miró's favourite café, and there is no better place for a quick pick-me-up.

PALMA'S HOUSES OF PARLIAMENT

Wiggle your way westwards over onto Carrer Colóm, then head south to the **Ajuntament** ❼ (City Hall) with a striking overhanging roof, supported by carved beams. Enter the street-level hallway and you will get to see a couple of ceremonial Mallorcan *gigantes* (giants) built of papier-mâché and hauled out for every local celebration. Further down the street, the magnificent ochre colonnades of the **Parlament de les Illes Baleares** ❽ have been the hub of city politics since the 13th century.

A hard left along the Carrer de l'Almudaina brings you to another of the city's original Arabic gates, the **Arc de l'Almudaina** ❾, which some experts suggest could date back to

Below: the Ajuntament.

Roman times. If you're hungry, the excellent **Las Olas** bistro, see ⑪③, is just up the road on Carrer Fortuny; great for a casual lunch. Alternatively, come back for a posh dinner at the atmospheric **Es Parlament** *(see p.100)* on Carrer Conquistador.

THE CATHEDRAL BY THE SEA

Head back down Carrer Palau Reial and the city's crowning glory, the cathedral known simply as **La Seu** ❿ (Carrer Capiscolato 2; tel: 971 723 130; Mon–Fri 10am–6.15pm, Sat 10am–2.15pm; charge) towers up before you (Seu means a bishop's seat). Like most places of religious significance in Spain, its first stone was laid on the site of a former mosque, in this case by Jaume I in 1229, and it took hundreds of years to complete. It encompasses a range of architectural styles, from the twisted Gothic features of the 16th century right through to Modernista flourishes added by legendary Barcelona architect Antoni Gaudí between 1902 and 1914. Check out his wrought-iron 'crown of thorns' – the baldachino – over the altar.

The immense sense of space and light here is largely due to seven rose windows, the most spectacular of which has a 12m (40ft) diameter. Externally, its flying buttresses give it a fortress-like appearance, while its watery surroundings make it seem

like it's floating out to sea. Take the time to walk around it, for it is truly extraordinary from any angle and at any time of day. The adjacent **museum** (same hours as cathedral) is worth a look too – it contains, among other curios, Jaume I's self-invented portable altar.

ROYAL PALACES

Next door to the cathedral is the **Palau de l'Almudaina** ⓫ (Mon–Fri 10am–6.30pm, Sat 10am–2pm; charge; *see margin*), also built on the site of a

Food and Drink

② CAN JOAN DE S'AIGO
Carrer de Can Sanç 10; tel: 971 710 759; B, Br, AT; €
Think regal glamour at this 300-year-old café. Settle into one of the velvet banquettes for hot chocolate and an *ensaimada* (the snail-shaped pastry sprinkled with icing sugar) on chilly days. If it's hot, you can get a scoop of almond ice cream to take away.

③ LAS OLAS
Carrer Fortuny 5; tel: 971 21 49 05; www.lasolasbistro.com; Mon & Tue L, Wed–Sat L & D; €€
A great local bistro that offers an excellent value, three-course *menú del día*. Expect creative Franco-Mediterranean dishes such as watermelon gazpacho and roast *bacalao* (salt cod) with apple *alioli*. Just the ticket after a morning tramping around the sights.

Above from far left: in the grounds of the Banys Arabs and a bathing remnant; the Basílica de San. Francisco is beautifully detailed; La Seu, lit up at night.

Bat power
Palma's coat of arms, as seen at the Palau, features a spread-eagled bat above the shield. Various legends surround its significance, but the most popular is that a bat flew into a drum one night while Christian soldiers lay slumbering. The noise it made woke them up just in time to save themselves from a marauding Moorish army, which contributed to their eventual reconquest of the island.

Above: tapestries adorn the walls of the Palau de l'Almudaina.

Moorish fortress. It was revamped by Jaume I in Gothic style and since 1985 has been the official residence of the king of Spain when he is in Mallorca. The 14th-century Capella de Santa Ana and 13th-century Sala del Tinell (Throne Room) are the principal highlights, along with some impressive Flemish tapestries. It also has a very pretty courtyard (Patio del Rei).

Shipyards and stock exchange

Head down the steps between the cathedral and the Almudaina, to what was once the royal shipyards. The site is now occupied by the **Museu Ses Voltes** ⑫ (Tue–Sat 10am–5.30pm; free), set into the city walls and devoted to works by contemporary Mallorcan artists.

Below: the lush S'Hort del Rei.

From here head back along the walls and cross over Avenida Antoni Maura to the Plaça de Sa Llotja, and you'll come to the whimsical-looking turreted **Sa Llotja** ⑬ (Mon–Fri 11am–2pm, 5–9pm when exhibitions are on; free), built by Guillem Sagrera in the 15th century as the merchants' stock exchange. Today, this elegant Gothic building is used for art exhibitions, a role for which its beautiful airy interior is well suited. Next door, the 17th-century **Consulat del Mar** ⑭ was built as a maritime court – today used as provincial government offices – and is easily identified by the cannon and a large anchor standing outside it.

A KING'S GREEN OASIS

Retrace your steps along Carrer Marina and Carrer Boteria (parallel to the Passeig Marítim), turning north onto Avenida Antoni Maura to the **S'Hort del Rei** ⑮ (King's Garden), a park filled with pools, fountains and shady greenery, among which stand several arresting modern sculptures, and a bronze *hondero* (the name of the early sling-throwers – in ancient times, Balearic islanders were famed for their skills with a sling in battle).

At the upper end, near Miró's famous sculpture called *Personatge* – popularly known as simply 'The Egg' – is a pleasant little bar with tables and chairs outside), the perfect spot for a nice cold beer at the end of your walk.

32 HISTORIC PALMA • MAP ON P.29

PALMA'S GALLERIES

Despite its size, Palma has gained a reputation as one of the most important art destinations in Spain. It has several privately owned collections as well as a few world-class galleries to rival those of Madrid and Barcelona.

Over the last hundred years Mallorca has become increasingly prosperous, a fact highlighted by its love of art. There are large galleries, outdoor sculpture parks and private collections stashed in stately homes all over the island. This tour covers Palma's big three.

ES BALUARD

The jewel in Palma's artistic crown is located in a former military stronghold, built in the early 16th century to protect the town against marauders. In 1952 it passed into private hands, and after a lengthy period of stagnation it was slated for destruction. A horrified public stepped in and eventually it was given to Palma City Council, who decided to turn it into a modern art museum, **Es Baluard Museu d'Art Modern ❶** (Plaça Porta de Santa Catalina 10; tel: 971 908 200; www.esbaluard.org; mid-June–Sept daily 10am–9pm, Oct–mid-June Tue–Sun 10am–8pm; charge, children under 12 free), which opened in 2004.

A local architect's firm, On Diseño, was commissioned to integrate the ancient walls with a more modern

| DISTANCE 1.5km (1 mile) |
| TIME One day or a leisurely half-day |
| START Es Baluard |
| END Plaça de Espanya |
| POINTS TO NOTE |
| This tour is great for out-of-season visits when the museums and galleries are quieter. The first two galleries are within easy walking distance of each other, while the Pilar and Joan Miró Foundation is best accessed by bus. You could also connect to tour 7 *(see p.48)* by hopping on the Sóller train at Plaça de Espanya and heading over there for an afternoon. |

design, and the result is a stunning contemporary gallery showcasing rotating exhibitions, that attracts big names from all over the world. It's worth setting aside a couple of hours just to appreciate the space fully.

Ancient meets modern

The original sandstone walls of the fortress soften the effects of the steel and concrete, giving it an unexpectedly

Above: Es Baluard is a striking building housing a collection of impressive art.

Palma's nights of art
With more than 30 participating galleries and museums, Palma's Nit de l'Art gets more ambitious by the year. It lasts from 7pm–midnight on the third Thursday in September. Entrance to all exhibitions is free and comes with a liberal dose of *joie de vivre*.

FUNDACIÓ JUAN MARCH

organic feel. Spacious and light-filled, it seamlessly combines interior and exterior spaces, encouraging visitors to interact with the building as well as the art within it. A walkway that wraps around the roof affords spellbinding views of the sea and city.

Above: artworks in Es Baluard

The 'Aljub'

The main exhibition space for concerts and installations occupies the former 'Aljub', a Moorish name for a freshwater reservoir. Until the mid-20th century it supplied fresh water to the entire Sant Pere district, channelled from the La Vila spring in Esporles along what is now Bonaire Street. Should you start to fade, the BLD rooftop café and terrace offer sweeping views of the port and serve decent coffee and light snacks.

From Es Baluard it takes just 15 minutes to walk northeast across the old city to the splendid **Fundació Juan March** ➋ (Sant Miquel 11, Palma; tel: 971 713 515; www.march.es; Mon–Fri 10am–6.30pm, Sat 10.30am–2pm; free). Weave up Carrer Olivera, through Plaça Santa Cruz and along Carrer Paz to Plaça Rei Joan Carles, then turn right along La Unió to the arcaded Plaça Major and north onto Carrer Sant Miquel, a pretty and highly enjoyable walk, which will land you in the 17th-century mansion Can Gallard des Canyar, now home to an impressive selection of the March family's extensive private art collection.

The March legacy

Juan March made his fortune in banking in the late 1930s, when he

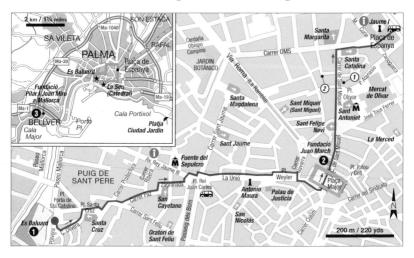

became known as 'Franco's Banker' after funding his right-wing nationalist party. His extreme Conservatism clearly paid off, because by 1955 he was seventh-richest man in the world, and his legacy lives on not only in the form of the bank which is still family owned, but in various cultural guises around the island.

Home of the Spanish vanguard

What is most striking about the collection is the sheer range. Dark expressionism by Miquel Barceló stands shoulder to shoulder with metal sculptures by Eduardo Chillida; surrealist and technical paintings by Salvador Dalí alongside big bolts of primary colour by Antoni Tàpies. These are just a few of the big names. At the end of 2010 a permanent space was inaugurated dedicated solely to Picasso's etchings. Allow an hour or so to absorb it fully, then treat yourself to a snack at **Cappuccino**, see ⑪①, or a more substantial lunch at **Misa Braseria Bar**, see ⑪②.

PLAÇA DE ESPANYA

To continue to the **Fundació Pilar i Joan Miró a Mallorca ❸** *(see below)*, head for the Plaça de Espanya straight up Carrer de Sant Miquel. Turn right at Plaça Porta Pintada, which pops you out on Plaça de Espanya.

Above from far left: exhibits in the Fundació Juan March; a lecture in Es Baluard; sculpture and canvasses at the Fundació Pilar i Joan Miró.

Food and Drink 🍴

① CAPPUCCINO

Carrer Sant Miguel 53, Palma; tel: 971 719 764; www.grupocappuccino.com; B, Br, L, AT, D; €

The Cappuccino group made its mark by offering top-notch coffee, cakes and pastries, alongside a solid wine list and a well-executed menu of salads, sandwiches and a handful of heartier main dishes.

② MISA BRASERIA BAR

Carrer Matias Montero Massanet 1, Palma; tel: 971 595 301; www.misabraseria.com; L, D; €€–€€€

Acclaimed chef Marc Fosh's latest venture is laid-back and buzzing thanks to a three-course lunch menu featuring fresh ingredients and an inspired à la carte menu with dishes like duck rillettes on apple remoulade and sea bass with roast peppers.

Pilar and Joan Miró Foundation

Bus numbers 3 or 46 take you straight from the Plaça de Espanya to the Fundació Pilar i Joan Miró a Mallorca (Carrer Saridakis 29, Palma; tel: 971 701 420; http://miro.palmademallorca.es; Tue–Sat mid-May–mid-Sept 10am–7pm, Sun 10am–3pm, mid-Sep–mid-May 10am–6pm, Sun 10am–3pm; charge) in about 30 minutes. it is a gleaming white building designed by Rafel Moneo, and the light in the gardens is at its most beautiful after lunchtime.

The prolific collection totals 118 paintings, 275 mixed media pieces, 1,512 drawings and 35 sculptures, covering the period between 1908–81. It also includes his personal collection of works by other artists and sculptors, newspaper and magazine clippings and other tokens of inspiration.

PALMA FOR FOODIES

Mallorca is establishing itself as one of the hottest food destinations in Europe, with Palma at the head of the table. This tour wiggles through the centre from the Santa Catalina market to one of the city's newest delis.

DISTANCE 2.5km (1½ miles)
TIME Half-day
START Mercat de Santa Catalina
END Botigueta de Sant Miquel
POINTS TO NOTE

Do this walk in the morning when market produce is at its freshest and you can work up a healthy appetite for lunch (on Sunday and from 1.30–5pm every day many of the featured places are shut). You could split it in two and do your shopping in the morning, before linking up with walk 1 or 2.

There is something thrilling about shopping for food in a foreign place, and Palma is no exception.

SHOP LIKE A LOCAL

The **Mercat de Santa Catalina ❶** (Calle Anníbal 19; tel: 971 455 079) occupies an entire block of the Santa Catalina neighbourhood. Rub shoulders with local people, learn about the fish and seafood and see what fruit and vegetables are in season. Shop for cheese and sausages and olive oils at

the richly laden Charcuterie Fausto Izquierdo stall; for *pimentón* and saffron, marcona almonds and pine nuts, go to Especias Crespi. To get really into the spirit of things, have a tapa and a mid-morning glass of wine at the bar with no name near Carrer de Soler exit. For something more substantial, the bars and restaurants that surround the market serve solid, unpretentious food, see 🍴① and 🍴②.

THE BEST OF THE REST

Cross back into the centre of the old town for the best of the rest. The most direct route is along the La Llotja section of the old walls *(see walk 1)*, left onto Avenida Antoni Maura and Carrer Conquistator, and left again onto Carrer Santo Domingo. Right at its head you'll find the **Colmado Santo Domingo ❷** (tel: 971 714 887), one of the city's oldest shops and purveyors of the finest *porc negre* artisan sausage in town.

SWEET THINGS

Minutes away, **La Pajarita ❸** (Carrer San Nicolas 2; tel: 971 716 986) is an

---

More markets

Palma has two other fresh-produce markets to explore: the Mercat de Olivar (7am–2pm), which is similar to Santa Catalina, and the early-morning Llotja del Peix (fish market, 6am) at Es Moll de Pescadors.

old-fashioned sweet and cake shop and the place to pick up a giant *ensaimada (see p.17)* packed into a cardboard box and tied up with string. The interior is a delight, with crystal chandeliers, Modernista tiles and a counter piled high with jewel-coloured sweet treats.

Continue along Carrer San Nicolás, turning right onto Carrer Mercado where the **Chocolat Factory ❹** (Plaça d'es Mercat 9; tel: 971 229 493) has an extraordinary range of products, ranging from truffles and bonbons to gourmet, single-estate chocolate and children's snacks. The packaging has won several design awards, making it the perfect place to buy gifts.

From here it's a leisurely stroll northeast to the **Botigueta de Sant Miquel ❺** *(see margin tip, right).*

Food and Drink 🍴

① APTC
Carrer Annibal 11, Palma; tel: 971 289 165; www.restauranteaptc. com; L, D; €€
A hip little spot filled with Santa Catalina groovers and shakers. The menu is more Pacific Rim than Palma, but the food is good and keenly priced, split into a series of menus and tapas for sharing.

② EL PERRITO
Carrer Annibal 20, Palma; tel: 971 455 916; B, Br, L, Drinks; €€
Popular for post-shopping coffee, brunch and laid-back lunches at the weekend, this place positively bristles with atmosphere. Try to nab a seat out on the pavement terrace where you can watch the world go by.

Above from far left: fresh vegetables at the Mercat de Oliver; La Pajarita is a must for classic Mallorcan sweet treats.

Organic and local
Go along Carrer Navarra to the Botigueta de Sant Miquel (Carrer Sant Miguel 79; tel: 971 710 505). They sell everything from fresh baked bread, organic eggs, fruit and vegetables to local honey, jams and delicious salt infusions from Es Trenc *(see tour 12).*

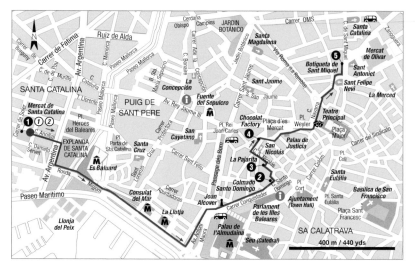

ANDRATX TO BANYALBUFAR

The southwest is a curious mix, where mass tourism meets the glitzy jet set then leads on to sleepy villages, terraced hillsides and glorious clifftop views. The tour can be crammed into a day, but it is best to stay overnight.

DISTANCE 33km (21 miles)
TIME 1–2 days
START Port Adriano
END Banyalbufar
POINTS TO NOTE
This tour should be done by car, but includes a possible boat trip and two hikes. It's best done in the summer if you want to make the boat trip to Sa Dragonera and swim in the sea, while spring and autumn are preferable for hiking. If you do plan to include either of the hikes featured, note they are fairly strenuous and not suitable for small children. If you plan to stay overnight, the Hotel Rural Nord in Estellencs (see p.95) is charming.

Picnic lunch
Wednesday is market day in Andratx. Instead of breaking for lunch, grab picnic fodder to take to the offshore island of Sa Dragonera or the Sa Trapa monastery.

This tour takes you from the swish port of Port Adriano to sleepy Sant Elm, then via a coast road with jaw-dropping views to a ruined monastery and the terraced hillsides of Banyalbufar, where there are some excellent restaurants.

PORT ADRIANO

To get to **Port Adriano** ❶ (Santa Ponça s/n; tel: 971 232 494), drive west along the main highway, the Ma-1, from Palma for around 10km (6 miles). Turn left for Santa Ponça and it is well signposted from there. Built in 1992, Port Adriano was handed over to French designer Philippe Starck in 2007 to be remodelled as the Balearic power port for super yachts (www.portadriano.com). A motion to extend it even further was recently approved, but for now visitors can enjoy its unique Starck design while strolling the docks admiring the pleasure palaces of the rich and famous. There are plenty of places to grab a cup of coffee before continuing.

ADRIANO TO ANDRATX

The Ma-1 continues northwards to **Andratx** ❷, which is spread messily out beneath the twin peaks of the S'Esclop mountain (926m/3,038ft). The town sits at the heart of a fertile agricultural region and is refreshingly

Above from far left:
Port Adriano; Andratx
is spread over two
mountain peaks;
delightful Sant Elm.

low-key in terms of tourism. Originally founded as a refuge for Christian settlers, it was the home of both the bishop of Barcelona and King Jaume I in the 13th century, and at the top of the town, above the Plaça del Pou, the towering walls of the fortress-like church of Santa Maria still stand proud and strong. There's not a great deal to see or do here, but it's a pleasant enough town for a stroll.

S'Arracó's colonial architecture

On the western edge of Andratx is the tiny village of **S'Arracó** ❸. Once said to have taken nine hours by cart to reach from Palma, it is difficult to imagine now, but the village retains its atmosphere and is good place to get a glimpse of the *casas de indianos* (houses built by Mallorcans returning from the colonies), now highly coveted second homes.

PARADISE ISLANDS

Continuing west from S'Arracó you will come to the pretty port town of **Sant Elm** ❹ – the gateway to the desert island of **Sa Dragonera** ❺. Once the hideout of Redbeard the pirate, these days it's the favoured haunt of a multitude of Lilford's lizards which enjoy lounging around in the sun. *Margarita* boat tours (€10; tel: 639 617 545 or 696 423 933), or water taxis (tel: 971 100 866) run back and forth to the island several times a day between May and September, and it's a proper paradise for those who can be bothered to make the trip – mainly walkers and birdwatchers who come to see the rare Eleanora's falcon and impressive numbers of seabirds. Scattered around are a number of little islets like Es Pantaleu, Sa Mitjana and Els Calafats, all of which are good for bathing and snorkelling. Remember to take a picnic, or head back to **El Pescador**, see ⓧ① *p.40*, for lunch in Sant Elm as you won't find anywhere to eat on the island.

Walk the Sa Trapa trail

Not a seafaring soul? Back in Sant Elm you can walk to the ruins of the ancient **Sa Trapa** ❻ monastery without leaving dry land. It's a popular walk and well signposted, but it's not suitable for small children and requires a certain fitness level – expect to take at least four hours to do the round

Walk this way

For keen walkers the most rewarding way to get to Banyalbufar from Estellencs is to walk along the cliff paths of the GR-221 (www.gr221.info; Mallorca Tramuntana Sud, Editorial Alpina provides proper maps to the region, priced at around €12). The area around Es Rafal has been closed for the past decade due to disputes over landownership, but a well-signposted alternative route was opened at the end of 2009. It takes a good day to get there and back, but it's an unforgettable walk with a couple of opportunities to jump into the sea at the start and finish of the trail. A picnic, plenty of water and sunscreen are essential.

Cultural centre
Check out the brilliant Centro Cultural Andratx (www.cc andratx.com), the largest centre of contemporary art on the island, set in stunning surroundings. There are also artists' workshops, a café and bookshop on site.

trip. The scenery, particularly when the spring flowers are in full bloom, makes your heart soar, and the views of Sa Dragonera are second to none.

ANDRATX TO ESTELLENCS

Back in Andratx, continue driving north in the direction of Banyalbufar on Ma-1. At around Km 99 you will spot the famed **Mirador de Ricard Roca** ❼, which has jaw-dropping views of the deep blue Mediterranean, providing you can see past the tour buses. It maya be better to bypass the crowds and keep going until you reach **Estellencs** ❽ (pronounced 'Es-ta-yencs'). The village is postcard-perfect, with narrow, cobblestoned streets and pretty honey-coloured stone cottages, their window boxes spilling over with geraniums and ferns.

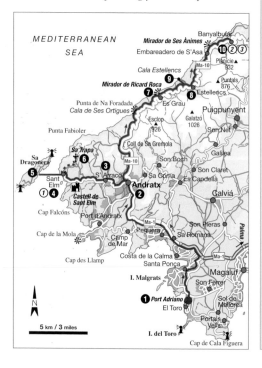

Food and Drink

① EL PESCADOR
Avinguda Jaime I 48, Sant Elm; tel: 971 239 198; L, D; €€
This simple seaside restaurant serves some of the freshest fish and seafood in the area, caught from the owner's own boat. The terrace gives views straight over to Sa Dragonera, and it's a great place to kick back and do nothing for a couple of hours.

② CA'N TONI MORENO
Port d'es Canonge s/n, Banyal-bufar; tel: 971 610 426; L, D; €€€
A short detour from Banyalbufar is this pretty shingle beach with one lone, inauspicious looking restaurant. The fish is first rate, particularly the *caldereta de lan-gosta* (a local lobster stew enriched with tomatoes and saffron).

③ HOTEL MAR I VENT
Carrer Major 49, Banyalbufar; tel: 971 618 000; www.marivent.com; L, D; €–€€
It's worth calling ahead to bag a spot on the spectacular terrace, which occupies a beautiful position on the edge of the cliff. The food here is simple Mallorquín fare for the most part, with Sunday lunch paella the star of the show.

Sunset swims

If you are spreading this tour over two days and have booked accommodation in Estellencs, end your day with a dip at pint-sized **Cala Estellencs** ❾. Take a hard left downhill onto Carrer Eusebi Pascual on entering the village, and follow it down to the sea (about 2km/1¼ miles). The rocky inlet and beach are ringed by tiny boathouses where local fishermen keep their nets and gear, and it's a wonderfully secluded spot for a sunset swim.

ESTELLENCS TO BANYALBUFAR

This section of the drive passes another viewpoint, the **Mirador de Ses Ànimes**, where there are stunning views of the coast from a 16th-century watchtower; along the route you get plenty of opportunity to admire the ancient terracing of the steep hillsides of pretty **Banyalbufar** ❿. On the surrounding embankment villagers once cultivated the now-legendary *malvasia* wine. Although the wine is no more, its name lives on in local parlance as a synonym for 'marvellous'.

If you arrive here in time for lunch **Ca'n Toni Moreno**, see ⑪②, does great fish right on the beach. And if you arrive closer to sunset **Hotel Mar-i-Vent**, see ⑪③, which was a chic, summer retreat for well-heeled Palma residents during the 1940s, is now a good bet for drinks or dinner.

Above from far left: the narrow lanes of Estellencs; picturesque steps in hilly Banyalbufar.

Below: the watchtower at the Mirador de Ses Ànimes

5

VILLAGES OF THE TRAMUNTANA

This beautiful, but relatively unknown region takes in some of the most spectacular vistas and prettiest villages of the Serra de Tramuntana.

DISTANCE 37km (23 miles)
TIME 1 day
START Bunyola
END Lloseta
POINTS TO NOTE
The villages are linked by the Ma-2110, which makes the route easy to follow, but the road is full of hairpin bends, so it's slow going. If you don't have time for the whole route, or don't want to rent a car, take the Sóller train from Palma to Bunyola, which links to tour 7. If you want to spend a couple of days exploring the area, Orient, with good restaurants and hotels, is the best base.

The pretty villages of Bunyola, Orient, Alaró and Lloseta can all be used as jumping-off points for a variety of well-marked hiking trails.

BUNYOLA

Driving into **Bunyola** ❶ on the Ma-11 from Palma, the first thing you notice is the striking yellow-tiled spire and bright green shutters of the Modernista Villa Francisca, which gives a sense of the bourgeois nature of these mountain villages. Known for its wine (the name is from the Arabic word for vineyard) in the 19th century, it was quickly adopted by the upper classes as an escape from the city during the Belle Epoque.

Salt del Freu
To get to the Salt del Freu, leave Orient following wooden signs for Santa Maria until they direct you towards the falls. You can also pick up the trail by continuing on the road to Alaró at Km 8.5.

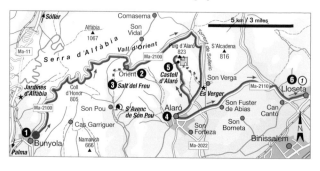

It is still popular with second-home owners, but has largely escaped the ravages of tourism. It's a sweet place for a cup of coffee, especially on Saturday mornings when the market takes over the main plaza. For walkers the the wooded glades that surround the town make for some good rambling. Paths are signposted from the train station, but if it's serious hiking you're after, continue on to Orient.

ORIENT

Leave Bunyola on the Ma-2100 with the majestic Serra d'Alfàbia rising up to your left. Once over the pass, the descent into the lush green fields of the Vall d'Orient is breathtaking, and the pint-sized village of **Orient** ②, presided over by the 16th-century Església de Sant Jordi, is no less lovely. Stop for a glimpse of the tiled depiction of Sant Jordi (St George) slaying the dragon before getting down to the serious business of walking.

The highlight is the mysterious trail to the **Salt del Freu** ③ – a 25m (82ft) high waterfall and misty river that runs through a forest of ancient oaks (*see margin tip, left*).

ALARÓ

Continuing towards **Alaró** ④, the road runs between two tabletop mountains: S'Alcadena to the left and the Puig d'Alaró to the right, with the ruins

of the **Castell d'Alaró** ⑤ perched on top. One of three such structures on the island, the castle is famous for resisting for four years the Aragonese invasion of 1285, and for the grisly fate of the two commanders in charge after they capitulated: Alfonso III had them roasted alive for their defiance.

The walk from the town of Alaró (3 hours each way) to the castle is one of the most popular on the island and well signposted. You can't drive all the way to it, but if you're looking for an easier hike, turn off at Km 18 and park at the **Es Verger** restaurant. It takes about an hour each way from there.

LLOSETA

Lloseta ⑥ is a pleasant spot to end your trip, with just enough interest to warrant a stroll and a poke around the shops. Don't miss lunch at **Santi Taura**, see ⑪①, one of the most exciting little restaurants on the island.

Above from far left: Bunyola's distinctive green shutters; the Castell d'Alaró.

Above: relaxing in Bunyola; a local crest.

Hotel Son Palou
Hotel Son Palou (*see p.96*) in Orient specialises in holidays for serious walkers, with many paths leading straight off the property.

VALLDEMOSSA TO LLUC

The central Tramuntana has long attracted artizsts, writers and musicians. This tour delves into their lives: from Frédéric Chopin and George Sand's cell in the monastery at Valldemossa and Robert Graves's writer's hideaway on the cliffs of Deià, to Mallorca's most illustrious scholar, Ramon Llull.

DISTANCE 54km (33 miles)
TIME 1 day
START Valldemossa
END Lluc
POINTS TO NOTE
This stretch of coast is far from undiscovered these days – come high season the tour buses and rental cars can be bumper to bumper. To avoid the crush, come in early spring or late autumn, or midweek rather than at the weekend. There are numerous places to eat en route, as well as a handful of places to stay, ranging from the luxurious to inexpensive *pensions* and basic rooms at the Lluc monastery.

Local saint
The Plaça de Santa Catalina Tomàs in Valldemossa is named after Mallorca's very own saint, who was born here in 1531. There are two shrines to her in the town, and nearly every house has a tiled picture of her on the wall.

Isn't it curious how different individual experiences can be? Sand's winter in the monastery in Valldemossa in 1838 was so miserable she was compelled to vent her unhappiness in a book entitled *A Winter in Mallorca*. Robert Graves had far happier experiences, pitching up in neighbouring Deià in 1929, where he stayed for the rest of his life. Indeed

it is largely thanks to Graves that the little village became such a magnet for writers, artists and celebrities. The monastery at Lluc, meanwhile, where Ramon Llull founded a school many centuries earlier, represents the most important religious and educational centre on the island.

VALLDEMOSSA

The truth is, **Valldemossa ❶** isn't as charming as it once was. Though still pretty enough, hoards of day-trippers from Palma have turned it into something of a theme park, albeit a fairly classy one. The main draw is the Carthusian monastery, **La Reial Cartoixa Ⓐ** (tel: 971 612 106; Mar–Oct Mon–Sat 9.30am–5.30pm, Sun 10am–1pm, Nov–Feb 9.30am–4.30pm; charge), where Frédéric Chopin and George Sand occupied two of the cells after the monks had been expelled in 1835. At least that is what was believed until a story broke in 2010 speculating that the cells purporting to be theirs were not, and the piano played during today's Chopin-themed concerts wasn't his either. Inevitably the story ruffled a

lot of feathers, and at the time of writing the dispute has not been resolved. What is certain is that Chopin and Sand stayed and worked somewhere within the confines of the monastery, and the Chopin concerts are worth attending regardless of whose piano it is.

Apart from said cells, there is an atmospheric pharmacy stocked with beautiful 18th-century ceramic jars, great views from the monks' gardens, and the neighbouring **Palau de Rei Sanxo** ❸ and municipal museum (same hours and ticket as for the monastery). The latter has a small but excellent modern art collection, including works by Francis Bacon and Max Ernst.

It won't take you long to get around either of these, so stroll through the narrow, smooth-stoned streets around **Plaça de Santa Catalina Tomàs** ❸, where walls are festooned with potted flowers, and stop for a coffee and the

Above from far left: in Valldemossa; La Reial Cartoixa; Deià has long been a magnet for artists, writers and actors.

Food and Drink

① ES PORT

Port de Valldemossa s/n, Valldemossa; tel: 971 616 194; L, D; €€–€€€

A comely restaurant spread over two floors with a pretty terrace looking back over the village and down towards the sea. The food is solid and unfussy, involving seaside classics like paella, steamed mussels, and interesting salads.

local speciality, *coca de patata* (sugar-dusted potato buns) in **Plaça Ramón Llull** ❸ before heading on your way.

VALLDEMOSSA TO DEIÀ

Leave town on the Avinguda Arxiduc Lluís Salvador in the direction of Sóller. When you get to the end of an avenue of plane trees the

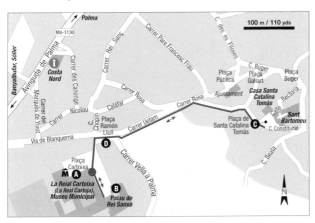

A fine *possessió*
Son Marroig (open Mon–Sat 9am–8pm; charge) is one of the island's great stately homes (*possesió*). It was once owned by the Archduke Ludwig Salvator of Habsburg-Lorraine and Bourbon, who installed a small marble temple in the garden, from which to gaze upon the pierced rock of Na Foradada in peace.

road curves sharply left for Deià, and with the first right you can head to the dinky Port de Valldemossa, a steep drive full of switchbacks and hairpin bends, but the reward is **Es Port**, see ⑪①, *p.45*, a good restaurant for lunch. From here the coastal Ma-10 is breathtaking, offering endless sea views to the left, and groves of ancient, gnarled olive trees among huge boulders to the right.

Son Marroig

En route to Deià you will pass **Son Marroig ❷** (Mon–Sat 9am–8pm; charge), one of the island's great stately homes. It was once owned by Archduke Ludwig Salvator of Habsburg-Lorraine and Bourbon, who installed in the garden a small marble temple from which to gaze on the rock

of Na Foradada, carved by nature with a keyhole-shaped window.

The **Mirador des Sa Foradada**, see ⑪②, nearby is a spectacular lunch stop, although the views are better than the food.

The Graves Legacy

Deià ❸ is set against the steep, rocky slopes of Puig Es Teix and is relatively lively for its size. There is little of note in the pretty, golden-stone village save for the Església de Sant Joan Bautista and its cemetery, the final resting place of Mallorca's most famous adopted son. The small flat stone says simply: 'Robert Graves, Poeta, 1895–1985'.

Graves acted as a magnet for would-be painters and writers (as well as established writers such as Anaïs Nin and the young Gabriel García Márquez, and Hollywood stars like Ava Gardner). Long after he died, the glitterati kept coming. Michael Douglas and Catherine Zeta Jones, Andrew Lloyd Webber and Pierce Brosnan all have houses nearby.

But Graves didn't just swan around being famous. He penned many of his great works here, including *I, Claudius*, and in the 1960s, together with his friend, American painter and archaeologist William Waldren, he set up the **Deià Archaeology Museum and Research Center** (tel: 971 639 001; Tue, Fri, Sun 5.30–7pm; charge).

In 2010 **La Casa de Robert Graves ❹** (Carretera Deià–Sóller s/n; tel: 971

Food and Drink 🍴

② MIRADOR DES SA FORADADA
Carrer Predi Son Marroig, Carretera Valldemossa–Deià Km 65.5, Deià; tel: 971 636 341; L, D; €–€€
Perched precariously on the cliffs, wind-buffeted and wild, this modern, glassed-in restaurant is an excellent place to drink it all in comfort. The food is nothing to write home about, but fine for a quick refuel or a cup of coffee. Its *fideus* (noodles) are popular with children.

③ CA'S PATRO MARCH
Cala Deià s/n, Deià; tel: 971 639 137; L; €–€€€€
Cut into the cliffs on a small pebble beach, with driftwood balconies, few places are more romantic. But the attention to spanking fresh seafood is such that it recently got the attention of Heston Blumenthal, who declared its Sóller prawns the best he'd ever had. Reservations essential.

636 185; www.lacasaderobertgraves. com; Apr–Oct Mon–Fri 10am–5pm, Sat 10am–3pm, Nov–Mar Mon–Fri 9am–4pm, Sat 9am–2pm; charge) was opened to the public. The house is as it was when he died, and it's worth seeing the short film made by the BBC about his life, then strolling through the gardens soaking up the tranquillity and landscape that inspired him.

For something special, it is worth the vertiginous drive down to the Cala Deià to eat at one of the best little fish shacks in Spain, **Ca's Patro March**, see ①③.

MONESTIR DE NOSTRA SENYORA DE LLUC

Lluc is the religious centre of Mallorca and home of the island's patron saint. The monastery of **Nostra Senyora de Lluc** ❺ (tel: 971 871 525; daily 10am–1.30pm, 2.30–5pm; charge) is a massive site, and a destination for tens of thousands of pilgrims. But it is of interest to visitors of every creed and none, for its history, for the architectural interventions of Antoni Gaudí who renovated the basilica, and for its boys' choir – the Escalonia de Lluc. Clad in blue cassocks, they are considered one of the best choirs in Spain and perform daily renditions of the 'salvo' – a chant intended to protect the island from harm.

The monastery was founded in the 13th century when a shepherd found a statue of the black virgin – La Moreneta – in woods nearby. According to lore she had a propensity for disappearing and reappearing again in the same spot she was originally found. After this happened several times she was given a chapel of her own, the Basílica de la Mare de Déu de Lluc.

Ramon Llull's school

Llull (see p.25) believed that the monastery was situated on a sacred site and that the magnetic properties of the earth were particularly strong here, making it an excellent place for study. He dabbled in all sorts of esoteric practices, but believed strongly in education, and education for the masses at that. The boarding school that was later established on the site is still considered to offer one of the best educations in Spain.

SÓLLER AND PORT DE SÓLLER

Sóller is one of the nicest towns on Mallorca, yet remains relatively undiscovered. Until the road tunnel opened in 1997, it was difficult to reach. In the 19th century it was one of the wealthiest places in Spain thanks to a thriving citrus industry.

DISTANCE 5km (3 miles)
TIME A full day
START Sóller
END Port de Sóller
POINTS TO NOTE
Sóller is a fantastic alternative to Palma, and this tour assumes you will either be staying in the town or the port, or taking the delightful wooden train from Palma. A car is not necessary, as there is a wide range of activities, ranging from soaking up the atmosphere of the Modernista town to hiking in the hills, to spending time on the beach at Port de Sóller. Both towns are popular with upwardly mobile 30-somethings as well as more mature couples. There is a reliable bus service that runs through other villages of the Tramuntana – http://tib.illesbalears. cat – from 7.30am to 8.30pm, daily, which is convenient if you want to hook up with other tours in the area.

Balearic gardens
The Museu Balear de Ciències Naturals í Jardí Botànic de Sóller (www.jardi botanicdesoller.org) recently moved from its perch in town to a more spacious zone just outside. Strong on Balearic flora with some planting from the Canaries and other Mediterranean Islands, it's a great place to start if you want to know more about what you are seeing when hiking.

In the 19th century Sóller not only produced large quantities of citrus fruits, but it shipped them straight from the port to Marseille, generally bypassing Palma altogether – hence the wealth stayed in this tiny enclave. Fast forward 100 or so years and the

imposing Modernista mansions and smart plazas are, if anything, more manicured than ever, while the completion of a multimillion revamp of the Port de Sóller in mid-2011 has given the seafront a much-needed facelift. Today, both the inland town and the previously rather shabby port attract boutique hoteliers, fine restaurants and smart clubs, where a more discerning traveller comes to get away from it all in style.

If you are driving, leave Palma on highway Ma-11, following signs to Sóller. The journey takes only about 45 minutes, a far cry from the nine-hour trip along the old road, which cut over the **Coll de Sóller**, before the tunnel was built in 1997. Although famed for stunning views back to Palma, the old road was, and still is, vertiginous and slow going, with 28 hairpin bends on the way up and 30 more on the other side.

Above from far left: catch a tram to the Port de Sóller; Sóller is delightful for a stroll; the oranges that made the town's fortune.

All aboard the little wooden train

One of the most enjoyable excursions on Mallorca is to take the antique electric train from Palma to Sóller, which departs from the *fin-de-siècle* station in Palma's Plaça de Espanya. It opened in 1912 and has been operating ever since, until the mid-1990s as the only comfortable way to get to Sóller. The scenery en route is lovely, especially in February and March when the almond blossom is in full bloom – a trip well worth making. Otherwise you will chug your way serenely through citrus groves and terraced hillsides until the train finally climbs over the mountains via a series of tunnels to descend into the orange-filled Sóller Valley.

Trains leave Palma six times a day (seven on Sunday) and take about an hour to reach Sóller. The only difference between the tourist train (at 10.40am and 12.15pm) and the others is that it stops for 10 minutes at the Mirador del Pujol den Banya to allow you more time to enjoy the tremendous view of Sóller, its valley and the mountains beyond, but the price is double that of the usual trip. For keen photographers it's probably worth the stop, especially if you time the journey for early morning or afternoon light.

Sa Fira I Es Firó

This lively festival in Port de Sóller takes place on the second weekend of May to celebrate Sóller's victory over Moorish invaders on 11 May 1561. According to local lore the town was saved by two *'valentes dones'* (brave women) who used the same bar they had barricaded their door with to kill their assailants, and successfully sent the corsairs packing.

Below: enjoying a sun-soaked lunch in Sóller.

SÓLLER

Even arriving in **Sóller ❶** has a certain 'wow' factor, since the railway station has its own art gallery showing ceramics by Picasso and a handful of lithographs by Miró. It's not a bad way to start a mini-break in the country. The imposing peaks that surround the little town would give it an almost Alpine air were it not for the huge swathes of orange, almond and olive groves that surround it.

Follow the tram tracks down the hill a short distance to the light-dappled main square, **Plaça Constitució ❹**, dominated by the church of **Sant Bartomeu ❷** (Mon–Thur 10.30am–1pm, 2.45–5.15pm, Fri– Sat 10.30am–1pm; free), its Modernista facade complemented by the ornate embellishments of the **Banco Santander ❸** bank on

the opposite corner; both were the work of Joan Rubió, who was strongly influenced by Gaudí. The church, in fact, dates from the 13th century, although the main structure is 17th-century Baroque.

Carrer Sa Lluna

Leading off the square is **Carrer Sa Lluna ❹**, a pretty little street of honey-coloured stone with a handful of boutiques and art galleries for browsing. It was so named not because of the face of the moon carved into the side of the house at No. 50, but because of the way the moon comes up over the mountains at one end of it.

Also in Carrer Sa Lluna is another splendid and extremely colourful example of the Modernista style, **Can Prunera ❺** (tel: 971 638 973; Mon– Fri 11am–1pm, 5–8pm; charge). This

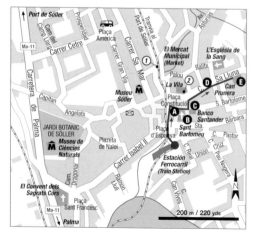

grand old townhouse, also the work of Joan Rubió, dates from 1911, and was a family home until 2006. It is a veritable jewel-box, featuring different, brightly patterned tiled floors, stained glass and an ostentatious spiral staircase rising up through the centre of the building. Many of the rooms, such as the dining room and some of the bedrooms, have been left decorated as they would have been during the Belle Epoque, but others have been given over to exhibition space for the work of a wide variety of local and international artists. There is an interesting sculpture garden at the back of the house too, and you could easily spend an hour or two here.

Sóller's other pleasures

Although this is the main sight in town, it is well worth a stroll around to soak up the atmosphere and, if you're lucky, sneak a peek into the walled courtyards and gardens of the splendid old houses. Remember to look up under the eaves – many still exhibit old-fashioned painted roof tiles that depict farm scenes and other aspects of rural life. Now would also be a good time to stop for a glass of orange juice, for which the town is renowned, for an ice cream at the legendary Sa **Fàbrica de Gelats**, see ⑪①, or for something more substantial at the flamboyant **La Vila Hotel**, see ⑪②, another Modernista gem, which serves an excellent lunch.

Port de Sóller

To get to the port, return to the town centre to catch the *tramvia* (tram) to **Port de Sóller ❷**. It leaves from the

Above from far left:
Sant Bartomeu has
Moderniste touches;
in the Carrer Sa Lluna.

Food and Drink

① SA FÀBRICA DE GELATS

Plaça Mercat s/n; tel: 971 631 708, www.gelatsoller.com; L, D; €

No trip to Sóller would be considered complete without stopping at this famous ice-cream-making factory. Although German-owned, this was the first artisan *gelatería* on the island, specialising in orange- and almond-flavoured ice cream made from fruit and nuts grown right here in the Sóller Valley.

② LA VILA HOTEL

Plaça Constitució 14; tel: 971 634 641, www.lavilahotel. com; B, L, D; €€–€€€

Although there is lots to be said for sitting out on the plaza watching the world go by, the real joy of eating at this chocolate-box hotel is the sheer magnificence of its decor: all floral whimsy and naked nymphs etched into pastel-coloured stained glass. If you prefer to eat alfresco there is also a secret garden at the back when you can dine in the shade of giant palm trees. Either way it's widely considered to serve some of the best food modern Mallorcan cooking in town.

③ REFUGE MULETA

Carretera Es Far de Cap Gros s/n; tel: 971 634 271; L; €

This is a popular stop for hikers coming from Deià along the old GR-221 trail, with stupendous views across the Mediterranean, a picnic area and the kind of hale and hearty fare required after a morning of walking. Think simple, traditional dishes at wallet-friendly prices. Booking ahead is advised, especially at weekends.

④ HOTEL MARINA

Paseo de la Playa s/n; tel: 971 631 461; www.hotelmarina soller.com; B, L, D; €€

Probably the most longstanding hotel in the port, the Marina has been run by the same family for four generations. During all this time, one of the highlights of eating here has been the authentic seafood paella that has people returning week after week from as far away as Palma just to get a taste of it. You can't beat eating at a table on the beach-front terrace.

Olive oil odyssey
Located several miles outside Sóller, Can Reus Hotel (www.canreushotel.com) in Fornalutx offers gourmet trips where you can visit a 600-year-old olive farm, harvest your own olives and make your own cold-pressed olive oil all in one weekend.

Below: the Port de Sóller lighthouse.

railway station and the corner of the main square and Carrer Cristobal Colóm every half-hour between 7am and 8.15pm, stopping en route where requested, and the journey takes about 20 minutes. The old-fashioned open-air wagons run on a line behind some of the village houses, allowing you to get a look at the small gardens, which adjoin virtually every house in Sóller, and you pass through orange and lemon groves and then travel parallel to the main road before entering the little seaside town.

The port has undergone a facelift, and as of summer 2011 has a wider beach than before, and a prettified boardwalk skirting the entire length of the bay. The tram stops every 100m/yds or so along the water's edge, allowing you to get off when you like. The first section – the Plaça de la Torre stop – is the best in terms of actual beach, a place to lay your towel and enticing waters in which to bathe. If you keep following the beach around to the left along Passeig de la Platja, you'll eventually arrive at the **lighthouse**, which affords magnificent views over the bay. There is a simple restaurant at the hikers' **Refuge Muleta**, see ⑪③, *p.51*, or back on the beach at the **Hotel Marina**, which draws diners from near and far for its excellent

paella, see ⑪④, *p.51*, an option for either lunch or dinner.

Santa Caterina

Continuing to the very last tram stop will bring you to the edge of the charming old fishermen's quarter – **Santa Caterina** ❸, always crowded with boats, some of which cruise (in the summer only) to the secluded Tramuntana beaches of Sa Calobra, Na Foradada and the Formentor peninsula. It is also a great place to eat *(see Restaurants, p.103)* with several good fish and seafood restaurants.

If you clamber up through these narrow, winding streets you will eventually get to the **Església de Santa Caterina** and the **Museu de la Mar Sóller** (Oratori de Santa Caterina d'Alexandria; tel: 971 632 204; June–Sept Tue–Sun 10am–6pm; charge), which provides a fascinating glimpse into the seafaring history of the town. In years gone by it was a magnet for pirates and corsairs, who were lured like moths to a flame to the lucrative little port. Even when the museum is closed, it is worth hiking up here to take a look over the sheer cliffs and inky black water below, imagining what it would have been like for residents of old when ill winds blew and their little town was in danger.

Above: looking out over the Port de Sóller.

Hiking in Sóller

Sóller is probably the best base on the island for walkers, and the ingenious Associació Hotelera de Sóller (www.visitsoller. com) is a good way to go about it. With 19 hotels and hostels in their collection, they offer something for everyone and every budget, along with useful facilities ranging from detailed topographical maps to guided hiking trips from February to June and September to October (some of them free). Through the association you can also plan trips if you want to go it alone, or organise a guide to take you through the Tramuntana on a trip lasting several days. There are, however, plenty of easy half-day and day hikes that lead straight out of both the town and the port, which are well signposted and easy to follow. The variety of terrain is spectacular, ranging from ancient cobblestoned trails put in by the Moors to coastal walks where the reward at the end is a jump in the sea, to rolling farmland replete with fruit trees.

8 POLLENÇA AND FORMENTOR

The northernmost corner is a great spot for families. Spend time mooching about the pleasant market town of Pollença and its port, and enjoy the spectacular cliffs and quiet coves of the Formentor peninsula.

DISTANCE 27km (17 miles)
TIME A full day
START Pollença
END Pollença
POINTS TO NOTE
This route assumes that you will be coming from Palma, although Pollença makes an excellent base for longer stays. The area has plenty of country villas to rent, complete with gardens and swimming pools – many of them more reasonably priced than you might expect – and many of the island's highlights, such as the west coast, Sóller and Palma, are less than an hour away. If you plan to do the tour in a day, Sunday sees Pollença at its liveliest, with lots of Spanish families enjoying their traditional lunchtime paella on the seafront in the port.

A Sunday market
Pollença's Sunday morning market takes over much of the old town, and is a great place to pick up local crafts, clothes, foodstuffs and traditional cookware.

Getting to Pollença
From Palma, take the Ma-13 motorway to Inca, turning left at the Crestatx junction, which puts you on the Ma-2220 straight to **Pollença ❶**. This is a pretty drive through rolling countryside, but avoids the twists and turns of the more dizzying Tramuntana roads.

The first sight you will see when coming into town is the abandoned hermitage of Nostra Senyora del Puig at 333m (1,090ft). It's worth making a quick detour up here for the view, before heading into the centre of town, clearly signposted 'Centro'. Park where you can and stroll along the Via Pollentia to the main square to begin your tour.

POLLENÇA

The central square, **Plaça Major ❶**, is where it all happens, with the tables of numerous bars and cafés spilling into it. It's lively in the evening with lots of people sitting outside to dine alfresco, while the surrounding side streets are good for boutique shopping.

But it is also a town that has several interesting sights. The 14th-century parish church on the square, **La Mare de Déu des Àngels ❶**, was built by

the Knights Templar and is one of several religious buildings in the town, including the church of **Nostra Senyora del Roser**, as well as the **Sant Domingo** and **Montesión** convents, all built in Baroque style.

The chapel on the hill

None, however, make their presence felt quite like the little chapel of **El Calvarí** , home to a doll-like figure of Christ that makes an annual outing on Good Friday. The reason for its fame is not so much about Christianity as for the 365 steps that lead up to it, one for every day of the year. Should you be in town at Easter, the *Davallament*, or 'lowering' of Christ from his perch in the chapel of El Calvarí to the streets below, is an impressive spectacle and great fun.

Pollença's galleries

The town's laid-back vibe has attracted numerous artists and it now has a handful of decent art galleries, among them the hip, modern space of the **Galería Bennassar** (tel: 971 533 514; www.galeriesbennassar.com; Tue–Sat 10am–1.30pm, 7.30pm–9pm, Sun 11am–1.30pm; charge), a nice contrast to the more conservative **Casa Muesu Dionís Bennassar** (Carrer Roca 14; tel: 971 530 997; www.museodionisbennassar.com; Tue–Sun 10.30am–1.30pm, July and Aug also 6–8.30pm; charge).

Skirt the town centre by car to Carrer Huerto to pass the **Pont**

Above from far left: dining al fresco in Pollença; climbing the El Calvari steps; the Pont Romà.

Summer festival
Every July and August the Festival de Pollença (www.festival pollenca.org) lights up the town's squares, churches and convents when they become stages for world-class classical music performances.

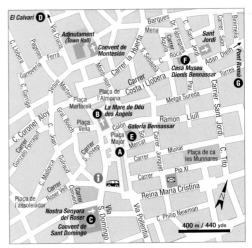

El Calvari ⓓ

Adjnutament (Town Hall)

Convent de Montesión

Barques
Mena
Sant Jordi

Casa Museu Dionís Bennassar ⓕ

Pont Romà ⓖ

Plaça de l'Almoina

La Mare de Déu des Àngels ⓑ

Plaça Martorell

Plaça Vella

Galería Bennassar ⓔ

Ramon Llull

Plaça Major ⓐ

Plaça de ca les Munnares

Nostra Senyora del Roser

Convent de Sant Domingo ⓒ

Plaça de l'assoleiàdor

Reina María Cristina

C. Philip Newman

400 m / 440 yds

A quiet beach
The **Cala Bòquer** is an isolated beach about an hour's walk from Port de Pollença. To get there, head for the roundabout at the top of Carretera Formentor, bear left and continue uphill past the Finca Bòquer (a private house) northeast of the town centre to put you on the path through the Bòquer Valley to the beach.

Romà ⑥ en route to the port. The origins of the bridge are obscure, but it is thought to be part of the canal system built by the Romans in the 2nd century AD.

PORT DE POLLENÇA

The bay of Pollença is shaped like a lobster's claw, with **Port de Pollença** ② situated right in the crook. It is lined with restaurants and hotels, many of which have been here since the resort's heyday in the 1950s, and is a good place to break for lunch. Options range from **Stay**, see 🍴①, *p.55*, one of the finest restaurants in the upmarket marina, to **Bahia**,

see 🍴②, *p.55*, for more traditional paellas and fish dishes.

The resort is bookended by the **Punta de l'Avançada** to the West, which you can get to by walking along the pretty **Paseo d'es Pins** (Promenade of Pines), complete with numerous pocket-sized, sandy beaches and little jetties dotted along it – all ideal for small children.

THE FORMENTOR PENINSULA

The Carretera de Formentor runs parallel to the curve of the waterfront in the direction of the Formentor peninsula. You can join the Ma-2210 from it, and soon afterwards you will find yourself climbing quickly to the **Mirador des Colomer** ③. The view down to the small island of El Colomer is simply stunning and one of the most photographed on the island.

From here the road dips and ducks through rocky outcrops and pine forest, switching from one side of the peninsula to the other, providing spectacular views of the Bay of Pollença and the Mediterranean. Be warned that it is a bit gnarly, and tough going for anyone who suffers car sickness. It is worth the effort, though, especially if you keep left at the **Hotel Formentor** ④, see 🍴③, and continue east through the woods towards the **Cap de Formentor** ⑤, the northeastern tip of the island.

Living the fabulous life

In the 1950s the Hotel Formentor was the place to see and be seen, and attracted a host of Hollywood A-listers such as Liz Taylor, Audrey Hepburn and Charlie Chaplin, as well as European luminaries like the Duke of Windsor and Grace Kelly, who all came to relax here. The beach is wonderful, with fine, powdery sand draped with low-lying palm trees, gentle turquoise waters and fine views across the bay. Although it's unlikely you'll rub shoulders with anyone super-famous these days, it's still a lovely place to kick back in the sun. Get here early for a prime spot on the beach.

Capes and views

On the flat stretch you will pass the crumbling old houses of Cases Velles de Formentor, where one of Pollença's most famous citizens, the poet Costa i Llobera, spent much of his life, and just above **Cala Figuera ❻**, in the distance, a lone pine tree, which inspired one of his most famous poems, *Es Pi de Formentor*.

Continue through the tunnels to the lighthouse. The views out to sea here are tremendous. The first headland visible to the right (southeast) is **Cap des Pinar**, which divides the Badia de Pollença from the Badia d'Alcúdia. Beyond that is the peak of **Cap Ferrutx**, and further towards the horizon is the headland of **Cap des Freu**. This is a great spot for birdwatching in spring and autumn, and on a clear day you can see Menorca, 25 nautical miles east. There is a café at the lighthouse, see ⑪④, which makes a good place to stop for a drink at the end of a busy day.

Food and Drink

③ HOTEL FORMENTOR
Platja de Formentor s/n; tel: 971 899 101; www.barcelo.com; B, L, D; €€€
If you are spending the day on the beach, the Hotel Formentor has a couple of options ranging from more formal restaurant dining to cheaper eats and child-friendly food on the beach. If you don't want to eat it's also a good place to sup a cocktail while you soak up the sun.

④ LIGHTHOUSE CAFÉ
Cap de Formentor s/n; tel: 619 748 591; B, L; €
A simple café serving basic snacks such as sandwiches and crisps, soft drinks, beer and coffee, and of course ice cream. It's not the sort of place you make a special trip for, but a fine stopgap if you're out at the peninsula and need to refuel.

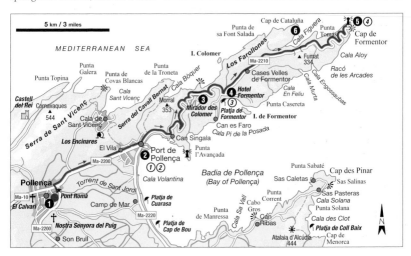

BAY OF ALCÚDIA

The Bay of Alcúdia is Mallorca's most popular family resort and gets extremely busy in high season. With lots of water sports, it's great if you're travelling with teenagers and also has child-friendly hotels and restaurants. This tour also includes a couple of tips for getting off the beaten path.

DISTANCE 30km (18 miles)

TIME A full day

START Alcúdia

END Colònia de Sant Pere

POINTS TO NOTE

The beaches here have plenty of family-oriented facilities, ranging from kiddies' play parks to water-sports outlets. The area also has several *ecovias* (bike paths) if you want to go on two wheels.

The great sweep of the Bay of Alcúdia offers everything you could need for a relaxed family holiday, while the ancient walled town of Alcúdia itself, and the Parc Natural de S'Albufera both hold plenty of interest when you want to leave the beach behind.

ALCÚDIA

Somewhat confusingly, **Alcúdia ❶** was originally the Roman town of Pollentia – why modern-day Pollença ended up inland isn't clear – and it later became an important Moorish settlement (Al-Kudia meaning 'town on the hill'). A good chunk of the sturdy walls of the old *medina* (town) are still standing, and it is well worth a look around.

The road from Palma brings you along the Avinguda d'Inca; turn right at the roundabout next to the walls (signposted to Port d'Alcúdia), and follow it round to a car park on the left, close to the remains of the Roman city, the **Ciutat Romana de Pollentia**, which was excavated in the 1950s.

You can enter the old city here, straight onto the **Plaça de Jaume Oués Prevere ❷**. The neo-Gothic church of Sant Jaume and a couple of small museums showing Roman and religious artefacts represent the bulk of the sights, but the main square, **Plaça Constitució ❸**, has some lovely Renaissance facades and some good restaurants and cafés, and the little town is a pretty place for a stroll, especially if you are there for the Sunday and Tuesday morning markets when you can shop for picnic food.

En Route to Port d'Alcúdia

The road to the port is well signposted from the main town, and on

the way there you may like to stop at the **Teatre Romà** (Roman Theatre). **Port d'Alcúdia ❷** is not wildly interesting in its own right – and it is very touristy – but it's a good place to have lunch on the beach, see ⑪① and ②, and puts you at the start of the bay proper. It is also the place to get a ferry across to Menorca *(see margin tip)*. From here, follow signs to Can Picafort, which takes you out onto the bay road. You can also walk all the way from the port to Can Picafort on a newly constructed boardwalk.

Food and Drink 🍴

① RESTAURANT MIRAMAR

Passeig Marítim 2, Port d'Alcúdia; tel: 971 545 293; www.restaurant-miramar.es; L, D; €€€–€€€€
When a place has been around since 1871 you know it is doing something right, and this top-notch fish and seafood restaurant in the otherwise touristy port is a gem. Service is excellent, views are fantastic and the food is always fresh and locally sourced.

② TRATTORIA DON VITO

Carretera Alcúdia–Artà 11, Port d'Alcúdia; tel: 971 548 074; www.don-vito.com; L, D; €€–€€€
A handy standby for pizza and pasta at the end of the day, offering a solid range of Italian classics as well as more sophisticated dishes such as *vitello tonnato* and *osso buco*.

Platja d'Alcúdia

The Bay of Alcúdia is a 10km (6-mile) stretch of beach sheltered by low dunes. The first section of it, known simply as the **Platja d'Alcúdia ❸**, is perfect for small children, offering abundant amenities, soft, powdery sand and shallow water. Its popularity means there's a good chance your kids will find plenty of new friends to play with too.

Parc Natural de S'Albufera

About halfway between the port and Can Picafort you will find the **Parc**

Above from far left: the 14th-century city walls of Alcúdia; birdwatching in the Parc Naturel.

Ferries to Menorca Iscomar and Balearia both run ferries from Port d'Alcúdia to the lovely Menorcan town of Ciutadella. If time allows, it's a trip well worth doing.

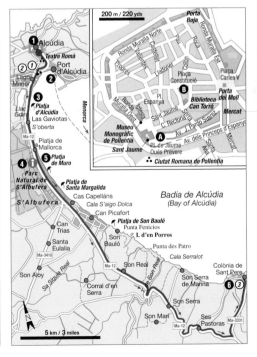

Above from left:
bright blue skies and powdery white sand at the Platja d'Alcúdia; looking out over Artá.

Natural de S'Albufera ❹ (Apr–Sept daily 9am–7pm, Oct–Mar 9am–5pm; free), an 800-hectare (2,000-acre) expanse of lagoons and marshes that is one of the best birdwatching sites in the Balearics. It is particularly magical during the spring and autumn migration periods.

Platja de Muro

Sadly, much of the bay is heavily developed, though it is possible to find pockets of loveliness such as the **Platja de Muro** ❺, which is part of the S'Albufera wetlands. It's a bit wilder than the beaches closer to the port and is a great halfway house if you want amenities close by without the crowds. It does have a handful of *chiringuitos* (beach bars, May–Sept only), which cater well for children and make a good lunch stop after a morning on the beach.

COLÒNIA DE SANT PERE

From Can Picafort the Ma-12 swings inwards, cutting out some of the grottier parts of the Bay of Alcúdia. Head back towards the coast just after Ses Pastoras on the Ma-3331, where you will see signs for the increasingly hip little surfer spot of **Colònia de Sant Pere** ❻ on the left. It provides a welcome antidote to the busy resorts, with its low-rise houses clustered around a small fishing port and a pebble beach. Round out a day on the beach with drinks and dinner at **Sa Xarxa**, one of the seaside restaurants here, see ❸.

Water sports

The Bay of Alcúdia is a prime destination for water babies, with activities ranging from sailing and windsurfing to kayaking, water-skiing to scuba-diving. Many places are geared for students, with courses ranging from a couple of hours up to a week. Most are open April–October.

Océano Sub Scuba Diving, Avenida de Mal Pas 1 bajo (in front of Cocodrilo yachting harbour), Port d'Alcúdia; tel: 971 54 55 17; www.oceanosub.com offers PADI courses for children and adults, as well as snorkelling and kayaking trips.

Sailing School Alcúdia, Puerto Cocodrilo, Alcúdia; tel: 971 89 71 03/651 890 954; www.alcudiaesports.com. Sailing and windsurfing experiences for first-timers and experienced visitors, with children's and adults' courses.

Water Ski School Familia Cartes, Platja de Alcúdia (in front of Boccaccio Playa, entrance No. 17); tel: 971 546 047/639 348 370/637 330 107/678 749 097. Offers water-skiing, giant doughnuts and banana flumes along with all the other paraphernalia of 21st-century life on the open wave.

Food and Drink 🍴

③ **SA XARXA**
Passeig del Mar s/n, Colònia de Sant Pere; tel: 971 589 251; www.sa-xarxa.es; B, L, D; €€€–€€€€
A laid-back terrace restaurant with fabulous views across the Bay of Alcúdia. Try sweet potato pancakes with home-cured salmon, or sea bass baked in salt with saffron potatoes.

ARTÀ AND CALA TORTA

Mallorca has a beach for everyone whether it's a secluded bay, a dune-backed shore or a surfer's hot spot. This itinerary is for serious beach babies combining some of the island's secret strands with an up-and-coming country town and lunch at a beach shack serving magnificent seafood.

To get to Artà, take the Ma-15 from Palma to Manacor and then continue northeast, on the same road. It's a straightforward route, clearly sign-posted all the way, although traffic can get heavy around Manacor, one of the island's main commercial hubs. Once you clear this, the scenery transforms into a series of low, gently undulating hills and lush agricultural land with the sea in the distance. The town has lots going for it, ranging from stunning architecture to excellent local bistros and good shopping, but it seems it just hasn't been discovered yet.

ARTÀ

Artà ❶ is hands down one of the loveliest towns on Mallorca, with handsome 19th-century townhouses, boutique shopping and an artsy community all looked over by the **Santuari de Sant Salvador d'Artà ❷** and surrounded by sturdy Moorish walls. It's worth the walk to get a bird's-eye view of the town, before spending a couple of hours exploring the backstreets in search of 'hippie-chic' clothing, designer interiors items and gourmet

DISTANCE 19km (12 miles)
TIME A full day
START Artà
END Artà
POINTS TO NOTE
A rental car is essential; there is no public transport to the remote beaches of the northeast. Try to catch Artà's lively Tuesday morning market (get there early, as it gets busy), and be aware that lunch at the beach hut depends on fair weather (they shut at the first sign of rain and all winter) – get there by 1pm for any hope of a table (you can't book). It's also a tour better suited to early birds than those who like lazy mornings. Both the featured beaches are good for walking (one on sand, the other on cliff paths), so it can be done out of season. There are some memorable places to stay, such as Sa Duaia, Can Simoneta and Cases de Son Barbassa, but early booking, especially in high season, is essential.

Club Ca'n Moray

Should rain stop play, check out Club Ca'n Moray in Artà. Non-members get access to pool and bridge rooms, a library, and free Wi-fi, as well as a top-notch restaurant and bar. It's all a good source of live music and other cultural events.

Above: stained glass church windows in Artá.

Manacor's pearls
There are few reasons to visit Manacor – the largest town on the east side of the island – other than to invest in Mallorcan pearls. Majorica (Carrer Pere Riche s/n; tel: 971 550 900; www. majorica.com; free) offers guided tours of its facilities and cut-price jewellery.

picnic fare. It's also a great place to eat: try **La Calatrava** 🍴① or **Café Parisien** 🍴②. Once they've discovered it people keep coming back, so if you want to stay here, book early.

A drive on the wild side

One of the great joys of this tour is the drive itself, out across the headland that joins Cap de Ferrutx and the Cap des Freu. A more different terrain from that of the Tramuntana is difficult to imagine: wild and barren, windswept and remote.

Drive out of Artá in the direction of Capdepera and follow signs on the left just after the petrol station to Cala Torta. This puts you on the bluff road that rises slowly upwards in a series of knobbly, windswept hills, more

Atlantic than Mediterranean, the antithesis of the snug coves of much of the rest of the island, that gives an immense sense of freedom. There's even somewhere to stay – the romantic Bar Restaurante Sa Duaia *(see p.98)* which sits isolated among the hills – and from where there are several wonderful walks across the headland. If you keep going, within 10 minutes of the road starting its descent you come to lovely **Cala Torta** ❸.

CALA TORTA

Popular among the surfing set, naturists and more independent travellers generally, Cala Torta is a scallop-shaped bay with cliff paths connecting it to other, still more secluded beaches.

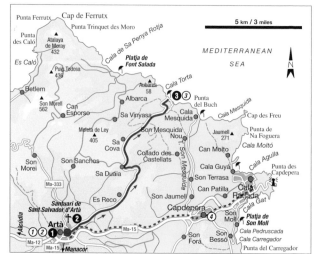

It's got a cool vibe, and the water is beautiful since it gets little by way of passing boats and there is no development whatsoever for miles. To the uninitiated it can seem a little brackish because of the sheer abundance of posidonia, a Mediterranean sea grass, but it's harmless, and indeed desirable since it prevents the beach from eroding. Unfortunately it isn't entirely pleasing to the eye when there's a lot of it washed up on the beach, but you can always find a clear patch for getting in and out of the water, and it tends to remain in the shallows. Seclusion aside, the other reason for being at Cala Torta is lunch. The eponymous bar is nothing more than a wooden shack on stilts, see ⑪③, yet it serves some of the best grilled fish on the island.

Live music and a cocktail

At the end of the day you have no option but to head back to Artà, but it's the perfect excuse to check out the bars and restaurants, some of which have live music in the evening. Café Parisien and Club Ca'n Moray are both good bets. Or head to Capdepera, which has a surprisingly lively scene for such a small place and some good places to eat, such as **La Fragua**, see ⑪④. Capdepera's main feature used to be its castle, which affords magnificent views of Menorca over to the east. Today, though, it is known for chic *agroturismos* and hip hotels *(see p.98).*

Both Capdepera and nearby Cala Ratjada are growing in popularity among more independent travellers. If you want to explore this part of the island both towns are worth considering as off-the-beaten-path bases.

Above: the glorious bay of Cala Torta.

Food and Drink

① LA CALATRAVA
Carrer Ses Roques 13, Artà; tel: 971 836 663; www.lacalat rava.com; L, D; €€–€€€
Part of the Club Ca'n Moray, this smart restaurant has a grand dining room with a fireplace for the winter, and elegant courtyard dining in summer. Think modern Mediterranean dishes, big on bright, fresh flavours, such as sea bream carpaccio with lime, wild garlic soup with shrimp, or maybe lobster with vanilla baked tomatoes and caviar dumplings.

② CAFÉ PARISIEN
Carrer Ciutat 18, Artà; tel: 971 835 440; B, Br, L, D; €–€€
Sitting here you could almost be in a bistro in Provence, offering Gallic and Italian-style dishes, jugs of fruity rosé and well-made cocktails. Nostalgic tunes take you back to another era, ranging from Bowie to live jazz bands throughout the summer, and it has a cosy, eclectic vibe that has you feeling like a local in no time.

③ BAR CALA TORTA
Platja Cala Torta s/n, Artà; tel: none; L; €€€
With just four small tables on a tiny wooden deck, and a pint-sized kitchen at the back, this is arguably the smallest restaurant on Mallorca. Yet those in the know travel from far and wide to feast on simply grilled, spanking fresh fish with crisp white wine to wash it down.

④ LA FRAGUA
Carrer des Pla den Cosset 3, Capdepera; tel: 971 819 403; L, D; €€
Should you make it into Capdepera, a stroll around the ancient battlements of the 14th-century castle should help you work up an appetite, which can be sated at La Fragua, which serves traditional Mallorquín dishes on a romantic roof terrace.

CAVES AND GROTTOES OF THE EAST

Mallorca has an extensive network of natural tunnels, caves and grottoes. Carved out by subterranean rivers over millennia, they resemble great man-made cathedrals and castles and are just as jaw-dropping.

DISTANCE 27km (17 miles)
TIME A full day
START Coves d'Artà
END Coves d'es Hams
POINTS TO NOTE

Although this tour doesn't feature any beaches, it links nicely with tour 10 (Artà to Cala Torta) and works best if you visit one of the caves in the morning and hit the beach in the afternoon. Note that in high season traffic can be very heavy on the Ma-4023 which links the caves on this route together.

The Jurassic limestone and karst formations that make up considerable chunks of the Balearic Islands are naturally porous. Indeed, neighbouring Menorca is nicknamed 'Swiss Cheese' among scuba-divers for its particularly porous coastal environs. Mallorca's best caves, by contrast, should be explored on foot, and currently there are six networks open to the public. The small but pretty grotto of Gènova, just outside Palma, is handy to have

up your sleeve for a rainy day in the city, but to get to the serious stuff you need to head to the east of the island. This tour explores the best three examples of nature's architecture.

To get to the Coves d'Artà, drive east from Artà in the direction of Canyamel, bearing left at the Torre de Canyamel. This road leads you straight down to Cap Vermell and the caves.

THE COVES D'ARTÀ

The fact that the **Coves d'Artà ❶** (Carretera de las Cuevas s/n; tel: 971 841 293; www.cuevasdearta.com; daily May–Oct 10am–6pm, Nov–Apr 10am–5pm; charge) are considerably less famous than their counterparts further south is a big part of their appeal: they are much quieter, especially if you time your visit out of season. Yet in some ways they are more spectacular. Less manicured than the prettified caves at Drach, the Coves d'Artà have a grisly history, which still permeates the atmosphere. Some 2,000 Moors hid in the caves after Jaume I's invasion of the island, but his Catalan troops smoked

Canyamel Beach
The nicest beach in these parts is Canyamel, a scallop-shaped bay backed by low-rise houses with just enough facilities to make it family-friendly.

them out, then slaughtered every one in one of the bloodiest massacres the island had ever seen. No one came back until the caves were 'rediscovered' in 1876; they are now reputed to have been the inspiration for Jules Verne's *Journey to the Centre of the Earth*.

Visits are conducted in manageable groups, accompanied by rambunctious storytellers who paint a vivid scene. The first thing you'll see on entry is a gigantic stalacmite – 'The Queen of Columns' – rising 22m (72ft) into the air. This is followed by the macabre

additions of the 'chamber of hell' and the 'chamber of purgatory'. Things lighten up a bit about halfway past the elephant formations and the 'Diamond Stones', but younger children can find it a bit scary. Tours last about 40 minutes. There are few facilities here, so pack snacks or head back out of town to the **Porxada de Sa Torre**, see ①①, located in an atmospheric 13th-century tower. Or, if you're looking for luxury, drive into Canyamel and treat yourself to a lobster lunch at **Cap Vermell Restaurant** on a jetty over the sea, see ①②.

Above from far left: the Coves d'Arta inspire wonder; the beach at Porto Cristo (see p.66).

Food and Drink 🍴

① PORXADA DE SA TORRE
Carretera Artà–Canyamel Km 5, Capdepera; tel: 971 84 13 10; L, D; €€–€€€
Decorated with ancient farming implements, this place oozes character from every inch of its ancient stone walls. The food is good, too, especially *lechon* (suckling pig) reared on the restaurant's own farm and slow-cooked over an open fire, and other traditional island dishes.

② CAP VERMELL RESTAURANT
Plaça es Pins de Ses Vegues, Canyamel; tel: 971 841 157; www.capvermell-beachclub.com; L, D, Drinks; €€€–€€€€
Probably the best restaurant on this stretch of coast, it forms part of a smart hotel (see p.99) with a magnificent terrace wedged between the sea and the cliffs. Eat grilled lobster fished from their own tanks, or stop for a glass of champagne.

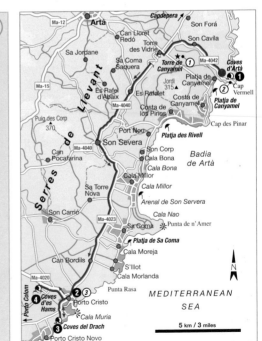

PORTO CRISTO

To get to **Porto Cristo** ❷, head back to the Ma-4040 and drive south to Son Severa, where a roundabout exit to the east puts you on the Ma-4023. This takes you straight into the town, the seat of Mallorca's only action during the Spanish Civil War, when a Republican battleship landed here with a force of 12,000. The troops managed to advance 10km (6 miles) inland, but the Nationalists soon drove them back, and things went quiet until the first waves of tourism in the 1960s.

A 1960s holiday resort

In its day Porto Cristo was a popular holiday resort, although the centre seems a little jaded these days, shops full of tourist tat and cafés selling chips having usurped the flavour of the place somewhat. However, it is pleasant enough and does retain a certain bucket-and-spade appeal. To get as much joy out of the place as possible, head down to the port on Carrer Burdils,

which runs parallel to the beach, down the steps to the fishermen's quay and follow the edge of the inlet as it snakes into town. It's not Cala Figuera *(see p.73)*, but it's a pretty enough place to stretch your legs, and there a couple of interesting architectural features to look at, such as the square at the intersection of Carrer del Mar and Carrer Sant Jordi (a good place to stop for a cup of coffee) and the church of Nostra Senyora del Carme in the square on Carrer Çanglada.

The port is also your best bet for a quick bite, with plenty of places serving simple, family-friendly fare at reasonable prices, such as **Taberna el Puerto**, see ⑪③. If you're looking for something special you would be better off going down the coast a bit to Porto Colom or heading for one of the more rural restaurants inland *(see p.104)*. For most people, though, the main reason to come to Porto Cristo is to enter the subterranean world of the **Coves del Drach** and the **Coves d'es Hams**.

Porto Colom

The less well-known little sister of Porto Cristo makes up in charm for what it lacks in size. Centred around two still-working fishing ports, it's a lovely place to have lunch and spend an afternoon strolling along the shore and soaking up the atmosphere. If you can, try to catch it during the Mare de Déu del Carme festival on 16 June, when garlanded fishing boats head out to sea in a floating procession dedicated to their patron saint.

Food and Drink 🍴

③ TABERNA EL PUERTO
Carrer Es Rivet 5, Porto Cristo; tel: 651 751 701; L, D; €–€€
Porto Cristo isn't the best place on earth for food, but the Taberna is generally a safe bet. Run by a friendly couple, it serves a good mix of family-friendly dishes and freshly made tapas, and has great views over the harbour.

Coves del Drach

The **Coves del Drach** ❸ (Carretera Cuevas s/n; tel: 971 820 753; www.cuevasdeldrach.com; daily 10am–5pm, hourly tours; charge) to the south of town, are Porto Cristo's main attraction, and understandably so. They have been tastefully lit to make the most of the intriguing journey that takes you nearly 2km (1¼ miles) underground, culminating in Europe's largest underground lake, where classical concerts are held and pretty sloops, strung up with twinkling lights, await to ferry you around. It's all rather romantic in its whimsy, and from the moment you enter there is a certain magic in the air, for these grottoes are straight out of fairy tales, full of mysterious shapes and formations, and weird and wonderful colours. All in all, then, a carefully staged experience, but one that has earned itself the reputation of being Mallorca's top sight. One word of warning: these caves get unbelievably busy and are best visited first thing in the morning or last thing in the afternoon.

Coves d'es Hams

Alternatively you can visit the **Coves d'es Hams** ❹ (daily Apr–Oct 10am–6pm, Nov–Mar 10.30am–5pm; charge), which are about 1km (⅔ mile) north of the town centre. These caves were discovered by speleologist Pere Caldentey in 1905 and feature more of the same, albeit on a smaller scale, complete with subterranean lake (called the Mar de Venecia) and a floating concert platform, with performances timed to coincide with the tours. If the crowds at Drach are too much, this is a useful second choice.

12

ES TRENC AND THE SOUTH

The flat, windswept landscape of the south makes it seem quite wild and isolated. Come here for bracing clifftop walks, to explore rural towns and pretty fishing villages, and to soak up the sun on secluded beaches.

DISTANCE 29km (18 miles)
TIME 2 days
START Sa Ràpita
END Cala Mondragó
POINTS TO NOTE

This tour is spread over two days. If you want to stay longer – and well you might – there's plenty of great-value accommodation, especially around Santanyí, as well as some sweet if basic seaside hotels *(see p.99)*. If you don't have much time, choose sections of the tour such as an afternoon at Es Trenc or a morning at Santanyí market, and make it a day trip from Palma. A car is essential – there is little by way of public transport to these parts – and the tour is better suited to couples or young families looking for an alternative side to Mallorca than parents with teenagers looking for entertainment, or anyone wanting to party. It's a good tour to take at any time of the year if you're happy to swap sunbathing for rambling.

Botanicactus
Botanicactus (www. botanicactus.com; daily 9am–6.30pm; charge) is the largest cactus garden in Europe, featuring more than 1,000 species from all over the world. It's a wonderfully tranquil place to while away a couple of hours.

The quickest way to the south coast from Palma is to take the Ma-19 to Llucmajor, then the Ma-5040 to Campos. The Ma-6030 trunk road heads directly south, and from here the landscape opens out into a series of empty plains dotted with acacia and broom, twisted olive trees and almonds, with huge, piercing blue skies and almost no traffic. No wonder those who have discovered it have kept it to themselves – when you hear talk of 'another' Mallorca, look no further.

Food and Drink 🍴

① CLUB NÀUTIC LA RÀPITA

Explanada del Puerto s/n, Sa Ràpita; www.cnrapita.com; tel: 971 640 001; L, D; €€–€€€
This swanky-looking place stands alone at the end of the port, but don't be put off; the prices are more than reasonable and the terrace one of the nicest on this stretch of coast, with excellent sea views. The cooking is likewise superb, offering spanking fresh fish and seafood, perfectly made paellas and service with a big smile.

SA RÀPITA

This tour starts in the dusty backwater town of **Sa Ràpita** ❶, because although Es Trenc is the most famous beach in the Balearic Islands, it is curiously poorly signposted. The easiest option is to go to Sa Ràpita and walk along the beach from there, or to follow signs along a fairly rough A-road to **Ses Covetes** ❷, where there's a large car park, which places you handily about halfway along **Es Trenc** ❸ proper.

THE BEACH AT ES TRENC

If Sa Ràpita is small and sleepy, with little going on beyond the recently remodelled marina, which does have

a handful of good places to eat such as the **Club Nàutic La Ràpita**, see ❶①, Es Trenc is a slice of old-fashioned beach paradise. With 3km (2 miles) of pristine white sand backed by low, tousled dunes, you could easily be fooled into thinking you're somewhere in the Hamptons, while the strong breezes that whip up can make it seem more Atlantic than Mediterranean. Rest assured you are in the right place, as pools of turquoise merging with sapphire-blue waters attest. Eco-activists saved it from development back in the 1970s and ensured that the entire stretch got natural park status while keeping it fairly off-radar from many of the island's visitors.

Much of its appeal is the diversity that comes with the seasons: it is great

Above from far left: sweeping sands at Es Trenc; find your way to the beach from Sa Ràpita.

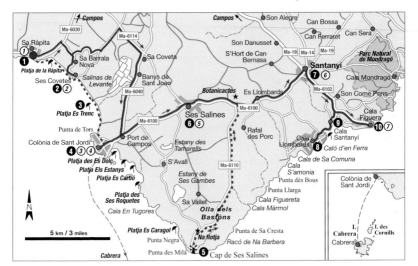

for refreshing seaside walks if you come out of season, while the central section is beloved in the summer by nudists who seek shelter from the breeze in the dunes. The water is shallow enough for younger children to play safely, while teenagers and grown-ups romp around in the breakers when the wind gets up. You will find a real mix of ages, nationalities, couples and families here, all with one thing in common: a love of unspoilt beaches.

Happily, then, it is blessedly free of modern beach-going parapher-nalia such as jet-skis, banana boats and other aquatic horrors. Facilities amount to a scant handful of *chiringuitos* (beach bars) dotted along its length, some of which rent sun loungers and Balinese-style grass parasols for the day, and serve basic lunches. The best is undoubtedly **Sa Copinya**, see ①②, and while you won't find Ibiza-style beach par-tying, it does have a lazy, laid-back vibe that keeps visitors coming back for more.

COLÒNIA DE SANT JORDI

From Sa Ràpita, drive back inland on the Ma-6030, turn right onto the Ma-6014, and then back down on the Ma-6040 to reach the dusty little backwater of **Colònia de Sant Jordi** ❹. Interest is growing in the place, mainly because it is from here that you catch the boat to the island of Cabrera *(see box, opposite)*, which is often, if somewhat ambi-tiously, described as the Galápagos of the Mediterranean. The town was established in 1879 as a centre of agriculture and fishing, and it wasn't until the 1950s – as in the rest of the island – that tourists began to arrive. Even then it was a very slow trickle, and although increasing numbers of hotels, bars and restaurants have opened their doors in more recent years, it still has the thrill of a place less travelled.

Food and Drink

② SA COPINYA
Platja de Ses Covetes s/n; tel: none; L; €

Situated midway along Es Trenc (about 20 minutes' walk from Sa Ràpita), a more charming, low-key seaside shack you couldn't hope to find. Excellent fresh grilled sardines and succulent fried calamari served by barefoot waitresses add to the air of bonhomie.

③ PORT BLAU
Carrer Gabriel Roca 67, Còlonia Sant Jordi; tel: 971 656 555; L, D; €€–€€€

This restaurant was opened by the Bauzà family back in 1965, and it continues to be a local favourite today. Buzzing with atmosphere, it's located right between the harbour and the beach and serves mainly Spanish seaside favourites like paella and *fideus*, as well as some child-friendly options.

④ ES PUNT
Avinguda de la Primavera 21, Cólonia de Sant Jordi; tel: none; D, Drinks; €–€€

This friendly local pub with a lively atmosphere is a great place to unwind with a few drinks after a day trip to the Isla Cabrera (they also have rooms if you want to stay the night). Food is basic, but most people come for the music – lots of funk, soul and occasional disco – making it the closest thing the town has to a nightclub.

Although it is no great beauty spot, it has plenty of rugged, seafaring character, and the seafront and port have been spruced up considerably in an attempt to attract the tourist euro. The shallow cliffs that separate the sea from the town make for a pleasant stroll before a lunch stop, maybe at **Port Blau** or **Es Punt**, see ⑪③ and ④. If you are around during the first weekend of August, try to catch the annual Colònia de Sant Jordi summer festival, when you will find the streets overflowing with giant paellas, free-flowing beer and cava, and abundant music and dancing.

Secluded beaches

Colònia de Sant Jordi is also the place to head for if you're inclined to seek out the island's more secluded beaches. Heading east away from the town along the sand you will come to several scallop-shaped bays – Es Dolç, Els Estanys, Es Carbó, Ses Roquetes, Es Caragol – each more lovely than the last, and ultimately leading to **Cap de Ses Salines** ❺. It's a full day's walk to get there and back (you can also drive to the lighthouse from Ses Salines), but well worth the effort if you're seeking solitude. Do note, however, that there are no facilities en route.

Above from far left: boats line the port at Colònia de Sant Jordi; the lighthouse at Cap de Ses Salines.

Isla de Cabrera

Despite its diminutive size, 'Goat Island', as it is called in English, has a rather dramatic history, starting with the Napoleonic Wars, when it was used as a dumping ground for French prisoners, nearly two-thirds of whom died here. It was also a favoured hideout for the pirates and buccaneers who terrorised the main island. These days it's an altogether more peaceful place. It was declared a national park in 1991, and nature-lovers will get a thrill from the sheer diversity of wildlife: there are seabirds aplenty, a chance of seeing dolphins playing in the surf, and an abundance of the rare Cabrera lizard, now extinct on the mainland. Once on terra firma there is a castle, a museum, a lighthouse and caves to explore, as well as some cute little beaches for swimming and snorkelling (the sea here is teeming with life). There are no restaurants on the island (there is a rudimentary bar), but lunch can be provided on board the boat from Colònia de Sant Jordi (€7), or you can take your own picnic.

SANTANYÍ

Heading inland on the Ma-6100 from Colònia, passing through the sweet little town of **Ses Salines** ⑥, which is good for a lunch stop at **Cassai**, see ⑪⑤, you reach **Santanyí** ⑦, which is the envy of other villages in Mallorca for its looks. The pinkish-hued stone used in the buildings here, besides being the most attractive of all of Mallorca's sandstones, is also the most durable and has been highly coveted at least since the Middle Ages, when it was used in such landmark buildings as Sa Llotja in Palma and the Castellnovo in Naples.

Southern soul

Today Santanyí is the loveliest town in the south, with a groovy, upwardly mobile vibe, thanks to the growing number of artists, writers and affluent second-home owners moving in, looking for a taste of the good life. It's a superb place to shop, with increasing numbers of boutiques selling high-quality goods like linen tablewear and delicate hand-painted ceramics, as well as several good art galleries, and a number of buzzy cafés and restaurants. It even has a decent live music scene thanks largely to the **Sa Cova Galeria Bar**, see ⑪⑥, which

Below right: Cala Figuera's charming harbour.

Food and Drink

⑤ CASSAI
Carrer Sitjar 5, Ses Salines; tel: 971 649 721; www.cassai.es; B, Br, L, D; €–€€
A hip little restaurant with a focus on locally sourced, seasonal ingredients such as grilled cod with aioli, stone-seared duck breast and mountain lamb with herbs. It also does good afternoon teas, handy after brisk walks on the beach out of season.

⑥ SA COVA GALERIA BAR
Plaça Major 27, Santanyí; tel: 971 163 146; Br, L, D, Drinks; €–€€
The unofficial meeting point of people in the south, Sa Cova is an eclectic little place serving international food like hummus and couscous, hosting art exhibitions and staging regular jam and live music sessions on Wednesday and Saturday nights. The music generally starts around 9pm and tends to go on late, so it's worth staying somewhere nearby if you want to join local people in these impromptu parties.

⑦ RESTAURANT ES PORT
Carrer Virgen del Carmen 88, Cala Figuera; tel: 971 165 140; L, D; €€
A jolly, family-run place that's big on crowd-pleasing classics ranging from tapas and sangria, grilled fish and man-sized steaks, stuffed aubergines and grilled vegetable salads, through to home-made pizza and pasta. It's a sweet location, too, with wonderful views over the port. Booking is essential.

hosts popular music and jam sessions twice a week. Saturday is market day and well worth a visit.

The nearest beaches are **Cala Llombards ❽** and Cala Santanyí. The first is a narrow inlet sheltered by tall cliffs and pine trees, with golden sand and a casual, laid-back atmosphere that suits Santanyí down to the ground. Throughout the summer sardines fresh off the boat are grilled over an open fire at a pop-up beach bar that also serves ice-cold beers to an appreciative crowd who sway to the sounds coming from the bar.

Cala Santanyí ❾ is more crowded because of the long-established Hotel Cala Santanyí (http://hotel calasantanyi.com), which sits right on the beach. But that means there are better-organised facilities and a generally more family-oriented atmosphere.

CALA FIGUERA

From Santanyí it is a short distance to the picturesque harbour of **Cala Figuera ❿**, which wraps itself around the high, limestone cliffs here. The first recorded data of some kind of settlement here goes right back to 1306, although it didn't develop into a proper fishing village until the 19th century. Park at the top of town and walk down into the harbour, which is one of the unmissable sights on the south coast. Lined by ancient boathouses cut into the cliffs and by pretty, whitewashed fishermen's cottages trimmed with green, it absolutely oozes charm and is a delightful spot for a walk, especially if you arrive as the sun starts to go down, and perhaps before dining alfresco at one of the many restaurant terraces that look over its peaceful waters, such as **Restaurant es Port**, see ⑪⑦.

Above from far left:
Santanyí is a delightful place to relax in cafes or do some shopping; fishermen's cottages in Cala Figuera.

Gourmet salt
Take something special home by choosing from a range of gourmet salts such as rose, black olive or Mediterranean herb from Flor de Sal d'es Trenc (http://flordesal destrenc.com). They are sold in delis and local food shops all over the island.

Parc Natural de Mondragó

To the north of Cala Figuera, the wetlands and cliffs of the Parc Natural de Mondragó provide excellent birdwatching opportunities as well as some great walks and postcard-pretty beaches. It can be entered on both the south and north sides, although the south tends to be quieter. It was afforded national park status in 1992 and now comprises rocky, wooded headland with lots of places for jumping into the sea and several pretty beaches – S'Amarrador, Sa Font de n'Alís (where the information centre is located, and therefore the busiest) and the more secluded Caló des Burgit and Sa Barca Trencada – which all have varying degrees of amenities.

FELANITX TO PETRA

This tour takes you off the beaten path and into some of the most obscure parts of Mallorca's hinterland. Travelling the roads that connect the remote sanctuaries and monasteries scattered across the island, you'll cross the market gardens of the plains and ascend onto high plateaux, taking in orchards and olive groves bordered by ancient stone walls.

DISTANCE 32km (20 miles)
TIME A full day
START Felanitx
END Petra
POINTS TO NOTE

This tour can comfortably be done in a day. Should you wish to, however, you can stay overnight in any of these simple monastic cells with nothing but the silence and the stars for company. It's a good Sunday tour, with a handful of pleasant hotels en route if you want to stay longer, notably Sa Plaça Petra Hotel in Petra.

Miquel Barceló

Felanitx has one significant claim to fame as the birthplace (in 1957) of the contemporary Catalan artist Miquel Barceló, who had his first exhibition at the La Caixa bank here in 1972. His work was immediately coveted, and he quickly began to show in other towns across Mallorca and the rest of the world. His most recent piece, significantly, was the Chapel of St Peter at the cathedral in Palma, which was completed in 2007, and which portrays, in ceramic clay, the feeding of the 5,000 and the miracle of the loaves and fishes.

Food and Drink 🍴
① RESTAURANT CENTRO
Avinguda Bisbe Campins 13, Porreres; tel: 971 168 372; L, D; €–€€€
An atmospheric lunch stop that offers a keenly priced *menú del día* of three courses including a drink, as well as more pricey fish dishes caught from the restaurant's own boat.

This tour will take you through parts of the island that many visitors do not see, where the beauty of the scenery is complemented by the peaceful nature of villages that time seems to have forgotten. The monasteries themselves are oases of calm, and if you have the time and inclination to stay overnight in one of them, it will be an unforgettable experience.

FELANITX TO SANTUARI DE SANT SALVADOR

Felanitx ❶ is not a wildly interesting town in its own right, although the church of Sant Miquel is impressive and there is a good Sunday market that is particularly strong in terms of local produce. It is also proud to be the birthplace of the artist Miquel Barceló *(see margin, left)*. Traditionally it was always known for its wine and brandy and it remains largely agricultural today, pleasingly devoid of the usual trappings of tourism. If you do stop here, keep an eye out for traditional terracotta water coolers, which have been made here for millennia.

At 516m (1,693ft), the **Santuari de Sant Salvador** ❷ sits at the highest point of the south of the island and straddles two horn-shaped peaks. The lower is occupied by an austere monastery, built in 1348, the higher by a 14th-century fortress, which alas is closed to the public. It's a rewarding, if steep walk (about 3km/2 miles) between the two: a good way to the blow away the cobwebs and a great place for landscape photographers to capture the shimmering early morning light.

Once back in Felanitx, head northwest on the Ma-5100 in the direction of the small town of **Porreres** ❸. Just outside is the tiny **Santuari de Monti-Sio** ❹ – worth a stop if you really want to the take the sanctuary theme to extremes – but it's recommended here mainly as a place to stop

for lunch. The recent pedestrianisation of the Avinguda Bisbe Campins sees it heaving with bars and cafés offering light snacks, although it's worth building an appetite for a heartier lunch at the **Restaurant Centro**, see ⑪①, before continuing on your way.

SANTUARI DE CURA

From Porreres take the Ma-5030 to the Ma-15 motorway, turning left shortly after to join the picturesque Ma-5017 road, following signs for the sleepy, picturesque village of **Randa** ❺, which is said to be the prettiest inland village on the island. The road snakes its way up to the tabletop mountain of **Puig de Randa**, passing stone cottages with pretty, moss-green shutters tumbling

Above from far left: Felanitx's Sant Miquel church features St Michael standing atop the devil; the Felanitx Sunday market; the Santuaria de Sant Salvador is spread over two peaks.

Above: at the Santuari de Sant Salvador.

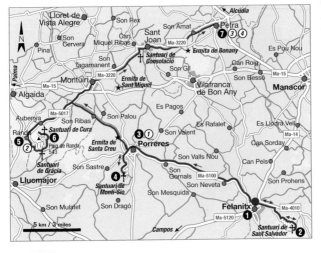

Sineu Market

A short detour from Petra along he Ma-3330 takes you to Sineu, an agricultural village, which on Wednesdays boasts the oldest market on the island. Dating back to 1306, it is the only one that still deals in livestock and is also a good place to pick up foodie gifts and high-quality crafts.

over with bright blooms, while tinkling streams go gurgling through. It has an otherworldly ambience, like something from *Lord of the Rings*, not least because the **Santuari de Cura** ❻ – set up by the godfather of Mallorcan literature, Ramon Llull, as a centre for learning in the 13th century – seems like exactly the kind of place a wizard would be proud to inhabit.

Ramon Llull's centre of learning

The sanctuary didn't become a monastery until much later, in the 17th century, and even now it oozes a certain scholastic air. Today it encompasses a small chapel, pretty gardens and a museum dedicated to the life and works of Llull: **Museu del Aula de Gramática Ramón Llull** (tel: 971 660 994; daily 10am–1pm, 4–6pm; free) Most visitors just come to admire the views, but you

Right: Petra wears its claim to fame proudly.

could spend the night (www.santuari decura.com) if you so desired. There are three oratories on the way up the hill, and **Es Reco de Randa** is a good stop for food on the way down, see ⑪②.

PETRA

Continuing north along the Ma-15, the road sweeps northeast through the pleasing little towns of Montuiri and Sant Joan (just past the Santuari de Consolació) to **Petra ❼**, an unlikely gem in the middle of nowhere. In the last few years Petra has become what you might call a 'boutique' town. Both the church and the museum, the **Casa-Museu Fray Juniper** (opening hours erratic; donation appreciated) are worth a look, but mainly to enjoy the pretty garden and as a means of placing the history of Fray Junípero Serra (1713–84) in context.

This Franciscan monk was Mallorca's most famous missionary, and one of the island's best-known sons. The fruits of his labours are particularly prevalent in parts of California, where he founded a number of missions, including the one that is now the city of San Francisco.

A town for foodies

It is the town itself that is such a pleasant place to spend a couple of hours and a great spot for foodies, with several excellent places to eat, as well as its own local winery, the **Bodega**

Miquel Olivera (Carrer Font 26; tel: 971 561 117; www.miqueloliver.com; visits by prior appointment; free), which has excellent fruity wines made by one of the island's few female winemakers, Pilar Oliver.

If you are having lunch in Petra, or staying for dinner, **Ca Sa Viuda** ⑪③ and **Sa Plaça Petra** ④ are highly recommended. Petra, particularly its cool and cavernous *cellers* – old-fashioned bodegas – is one of the best places on the island for *cuina Mallorquina*, traditional country cooking.

Above from far left: an unbeatable view for lunch from the Santuari de Cura on Puig de Randa; precious religious manuscripts in Petra.

Food and Drink

② ES RECO DE RANDA
Carrer Font 21, Randa; tel: 971 120 302; www.esreco deranda.com; L, D; €–€€€
A pretty, 17th-century inn that is especially good on a chilly day in winter, when they light the fire in the dining room. Expect to find hearty country classics such as wood-roasted suckling pig and *arroz brut* (clay-pot rice).

③ CA SA VIUDA
Carrer Pou 35, Petra; tel: 971 830 100; L, D; €–€€
The 'House of the Widow' is a sweet little place, where you will find authentic island cooking (*cuina Mallorquina*) such as fried liver and kidneys, roast meats and rib-sticking stews. It is super-friendly and serves enormous portions. It's a great place to come after a long day's sightseeing or walking, but be warned that you want to come here really hungry.

④ SA PLAÇA PETRA
Sa Plaça 4, Petra; tel: 971 561 646; L, D; €€–€€€
This is one of the area's more upmarket restaurants. Sa Plaça has quaint, country-cottage decor and serves staunchly traditional fare. You will be offered dishes such as crayfish and chocolate (try it, it sounds like a strange combination, but is very good) and chicken stuffed with prawns. But do try to save room to savour some of their delectable home-made puddings.

WINE COUNTRY

Mallorca is fast making its mark as a serious winemaking region, much of it centred around the rural town of Binissalem, a good base for visiting some of the best and most exciting wineries and getting to grips with the endemic grape varieties while doing some pleasant sipping and swirling.

DISTANCE 25km (15 miles)

TIME A full day

START Santa Maria del Camí

END Binissalem

POINTS TO NOTE

This tour is created for driving, but it could easily be done by bicycle since distances are short and the region is flat. The best time of year to do it is September, when the grape harvest celebrations take place, but if you find yourself here in August, the Bodega Vins Nadal hosts a super jazz festival. With 13 different wineries – details of which can be seen at www.binissalem do.com – now open to the public, you could easily make the tour last a few days or a long weekend. This route takes in a broad selection to serve as a general introduction to the area.

Local varieties

The most important local grape varieties are Manto Negro, Callet and Moll (red) and Premsal Blanco (white). Look out for these on the bottle labels to get a proper taste of Mallorca's distinctive *terroir*.

Wine has been made on Mallorca since Roman times, and the vintages were highly regarded, too, compared by the historian Pliny to the finest wines in Italy. Over time the production of wine spread across the island into the regions of Bunyola, Campos, Felanitx, Manacor, Porreres and Valldemossa, although much of it was wiped out during the phyloxera outbreak in 1899. Up until this point, and unlike the rest of Europe, the island had remained blessedly free of the wine louse, but in the following 100 years production fell from 30,000 hectares (75,000 acres) to a mere 2,000 (5,000). It wasn't until the 1960s that wine production started up in earnest again, and as interest in Spain as a gourmet destination grew in the mid-1990s, so winemakers in Mallorca upped their game. Today they offer some of the most exciting (and expensive) wines in the country, and there is no better place to get acquainted with them.

SANTA MARIA DEL CAMÍ

Away from the coasts, the quiet countryside and ancient towns of the Mallorcan interior have remained largely unaffected by tourism, offering a taste of old-style island life to those who make the effort to go and find it. Take the Ma-13 highway from Palma

in the direction of Inca, and within 15 minutes you will see signs to the pretty village of **Santa Maria del Camí** ❶ – a good place to fuel up with a strong cup of coffee in the main square before this tour begins.

Macià Batle ❷ (Camí de Coanegra s/n, Santa Maria del Camí; tel: 971 140 014; www.maciabatle.com) is located just a little way north of the town centre, and is one of Mallorca's best-known wineries, occupying an impressive position on the plains, with the Tramuntana mountain range rising up behind. The winery is well geared for visits, with a smart new tasting room that looks out over the maceration tanks and the vineyards, but the labels themselves are also noteworthy, as each has been designed by a famous artist – both international names and local ones – among them Rebecca Horn, Yannick Vu and Pep Coll.

At the other end of the scale, **Celler Sebastià Pastor** ❸ (Carrer Paborde Jaume 17, Santa Maria del Camí; tel: 971 620 358) is a far more modest affair, but interesting because here they make wines using only local grape varieties. The wine is simple – table wines rather than great vintages – but an enjoyable quaffer that is perfect for picnics.

SENCELLES

On the road to Sencelles you will pass **Bodegas Angel** ❹ (Carretera Santa Maria–Sencelles Km 4.8; tel: 971 621 638; www.bodegasangel.com), one of the most state-of-the art, modern wineries on the island, which prides

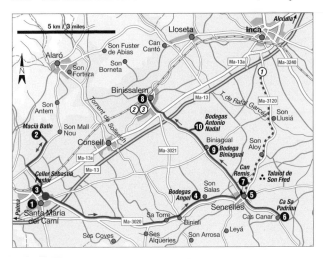

itself on excellent new-wave wines, including a stupendous white. For anyone who appreciates small production boutique wines, this is one not to be missed.

Continue in the direction of the one-horse town of **Sencelles** ❺ and just outside you will find **Ca Sa Padrina** ❻ (Cami dels Horts s/n, Sencelles; tel: 686 933 991), which is likewise intent on rediscovering traditional winemaking techniques by using only endemic grape varieties and harvesting everything by hand. Again, it's a must for serious wine drinkers.

A truly traditional winery

Heading directly north out of town, **Can Remis** ❼ (Carrer Sor Francinaina Ana Cirer 14, Sencelles; tel: 971 872 418) is one of the oldest

wineries and brandy distillers on the island, dating back to 1870. It makes a striking contrast to the more contemporary facilities you will have visited earlier in the day, and is a good halfway point for breaking for lunch. It's a bit of a detour, but worth travelling the few extra kilometres along the old Inca road to **Son Aloy**, see ⑪①, a fine place for lunch among the vines (and you could easily loop back to Binissalem from here on the fast Ma-13 highway).

BINISSALEM

If you are happy to keep going, continue north to **Binissalem** ❽, which has several good eating options and puts you at the heart of wine-growing country. But be sure to save enough

Celler restaurants

Most of what you read about Inca is in the context of its leather-working past and its current incarnation as a hub of shoe outlets. The truth is both industries are in decline, and bargains are few and far between. Inca, in fact, is far more interesting as the centre of centuries-old wine *cellers*, which operated much like modern-day wine bars. Most didn't start serving food until the mid-20th century, but once they did, a whole new tradition of *celler* cuisine was born: one that was hale and hearty, featuring local produce in abundance, and restored regional recipes such as roast quail and pork wrapped in cabbage leaves to their place at the top of the island's culinary hierarchy. Come to Inca to eat rather than shop, and you won't leave disappointed.

energy to stop en route at the **Bodega Biniagual** ❾ (Llogaret de Biniagual; tel: 971 511 524; www.bodegabiniagual. com), arguably the prettiest winery on the island. The cooperative occupies the whole hamlet of Biniagual and attracts some of Spain's most talented winemakers, so it always makes for interesting drinking.

Just before you reach town, **Bodegas Antonio Nadal** ❿ (Finca Son Roig, Camí de Son Roig, Binissalem; tel: 639 660 945; www.bodegasantonionadal. com) was the first winery on the island to gain D.O. status back in 1989. Its wines are still considered to be among the best, and if you treat yourself to a bottle of Magdalena Nadal Estela you will find out why.

And so to Binissalem, the official seat of the D.O. (Denominación de Origen). **Vins Nadal** (Carrer Ramon Llull 2, Binissalem; tel: 971 511 058; www.vinsnadal.com) offers consistently high-quality wines at reasonable prices. They also stage jazz concerts in the cellars in the summer, combining great food, wine and music. It's well worth bagging a ticket for these if you can (see the website for details). But no visit is complete without stopping at **José Luis Ferrer** (Carrer Conquistador 103; tel: 971 511 050; www. vinosferrer.com), probably the island's most famous winery. The distinctive orange label of their crianza is the house wine of choice for restaurants all over Mallorca.

Thus lubricated, you will be glad to know there are several good places to eat in Binissalem, and it's a great place to round off the day either with a full dinner or with drinks on the square: try **Café Singló** or **La Salamandra**, see ⑪② and ③.

Food and Drink 🍴

① CELLER SON ALOY

Carretera Inca–Sencelles Km 3; tel: 971 88 38 24; L, D; €€
Set amid the vineyards of Sencelles, this is a lovely place to dine alfresco in the summer and well worth the detour. The specials here are snails from the vineyards and *bacalao* (salt cod) done in a myriad of different ways, although a firm favourite is *sobrassada* (*pimentón*-spiced pork sausage) and honey.

② CAFÉ SINGLÓ

Plaça Església 5, Binissalem; tel: 971 870 599; B, L, D; €–€€
This upmarket café with a pleasant terrace on the main square is very much a local meeting point, whether it's for coffee first thing in the morning, a top-flight three-course *menú* for lunch, or drinks in the evening.

③ LA SALAMANDRA

Carrer de Pou Bo 20, Binissalem; tel: 971 870 076; L, D; €–€€
Recently opened by the son of the owners of Scott's boutique hotel, La Salamandra serves light bites such as freshly made sandwiches, salads and soups, as well as a handful of daily specials chalked up on the blackboard.

Above from far left: Bodegas Angel's vineyard; local Rioja; start your tour of the wine country in Santa Maria del Camí.

More wine routes If you've got the wine route bug you could also check out the boutique bodegas of Anima Negra and 4Kilos in Felanitx in the southeast corner of the island *(see tour 13, p.74).*

DIRECTORY

A user-friendly alphabetical listing of practical information, plus hand-picked hotels and restaurants, clearly organised by area, to suit all budgets and tastes. Select nightlife listings are also included here.

A

AGE RESTRICTIONS

The age of consent in Spain is 13 for both heterosexual and homosexual sex. You can drive a small moped at 14, and smoke and drink from age 16. To drive a car or motorbike over 125cc you need to be over 18.

B

BUDGETING

A *caña* (small draught beer): €1.60
Glass of house wine: €1.60
Main course: budget restaurant €7.90, mid-range €15, expensive €21+
Hotels: budget €45, moderate €80, de luxe €350+
Taxi from Palma airport to city centre: €24
A single bus ticket: €1.10

C

CHILDREN

The Spanish adore kids. Even fairly late at night, you will find that restaurants welcome little ones with open arms, and most serve child-friendly meals. Nearly all sights and theme parks offer a discount for under-12s, and resort hotels are generally pretty good when it comes to children's activities.

CLIMATE

Mid-June until September is virtually rainless, with wall-to-wall sunshine. In July, the hottest month, temperatures range from 30°C (86°F) in the afternoon to about 20°C (68°F) at night. Autumn temperatures are typically around 24°C (75°F), but there are often short heavy rains in early September; October is the wettest month. April and May see a little rain with lots of sunshine and moderate temperatures. In winter, expect some rain and cool winds, but most days are sunny, and it is usually warm enough at midday to sit outside. Average maximum/minimum winter temperatures are 15°C (59°F) and 7°C (45°F).

CLOTHING

Mallorca is pretty low-key, though older people dress up a bit for their evening *paseo* (promenade); a T-shirt and shorts are the minimum requirement for both men and women. Never wear beach gear in towns (you can now be fined for this), and when visiting churches cover your shoulders and knees. Going topless on the beaches is fairly normal, though total nudity should be kept to designated beaches.

In spring and autumn bring lots of light layers and a mac. In summer you won't need much more than something to cover up with, but bring something warm and waterproof in the winter.

CRIME AND SAFETY

Mallorca is generally pretty safe and serious crime extremely rare. Employ the same precautions you would anywhere, though: keep your eye on your purse and camera at all times, especially in crowded areas, and take care when withdrawing money from ATMs. Leave valuables in the hotel safe; make a photocopy of your passport and carry it with you. If you hire a car, don't leave property visible inside.

If any of your property is lost or stolen you must report it to the police within 24 hours if you intend to make a claim on your insurance policy.

CUSTOMS

EU nationals may purchase up to 800 cigarettes, 200 cigars or 1kg tobacco, 10l of spirits and 90l of wine. Non-EU nationals may purchase 200 cigarettes, 50 cigars, 250g loose tobacco, 1l spirits and 2l wine.

DISABLED TRAVELERS

If travelling with a wheelchair, inform the airline or ferry service in advance. Help is always on hand for getting through arrival and departure halls. Not all bars, restaurants or hotels are equipped with ramps or lifts, so check the facilities in advance.

ELECTRICITY

220 volts AC. British appliances work perfectly well but need an adaptor, as sockets are the two round-pin type; US appliances need a transformer.

EMBASSIES AND CONSULATES

Australia: in Madrid at Plaza del Descubridor Diego de Ordas 3; tel: 914 419 300.
Canada: in Madrid at Torre Espacio, Paseo de la Castellana 259; tel: 913 828 400.
Ireland: Carrer Sant Miquel 68, Palma; tel: 971 719 244.
UK: Carrer Convent dels Caputxins 4, Edificio Orisba B; tel: 902 109 356/971 712 445, www.fco.gov.uk.
US: Edificio Reina Constanza, Carrer Porto Pi 8, 9th floor, Palma; tel: 971 403 707.

EMERGENCIES

Police, fire, ambulance: 112
Policía Nacional: 091
Policía Municipal: 092
Guardia Civil (traffic): 062

ETIQUETTE

Islanders are easy-going people, but be respectful of their religion, dress

sensibly in towns and cities and learn a couple of words of Catalan for exchanging niceties in the street. Above all, be open – people are friendly and curious about foreign visitors.

F

FESTIVALS

Most towns and villages have a local festival celebrating their patron saint, which incorporate abundant dancing, eating and drinking. The most interesting have appearances by *cavallets* – dancers with cardboard hobby-horses strapped to them – and *dimoni* – red-clad devils. Highlights include: Palma's carnival in February; Semana Santa (Holy Week) in Pollença; Cristianos i Morus in Sóller on 8–10 May; festivals of classical music in Pollença and Deià throughout July and August; Festa des Vermar (Wine Festival) on the last Sunday of September in Binissalem. Check www.illesbalears.es/ing/balearicislands/festivals for a list of other events.

FURTHER READING

General background
Tuning up at Dawn by Tomàs Graves (Fourth Estate). Robert Graves's son writes about life and music.
Wild Olives by William Graves (Hutchinson). Robert Graves's other son's account of growing up in Deià.

Walking/climbing/birdwatching
Walking in Mallorca by June Parker (Cicerone Press). Detail of more than 70 hikes all over the island.
Birdwatching in Mallorca by Ken Stoba (Cicerone). Catalogue of birdlife and sites.

Food
The Taste of a Place: Mallorca by Vicky Bennison (Chakula Press). A mouth-watering introduction to Mallorcan food.
Bread and Oil by Tomàs Graves (Univ. of Wisconsin Press). An insider's look at two of Mallorca's great products.

Travel accounts
A Winter in Majorca by George Sand (Valldemossa Editions). Sand's scathing account of her stay on the island in 1838–9 with Chopin (translated by Robert Graves).

Fiction
The Bloody Bokhara by George Scott (Eye Level Books). Mallorcan murder mystery, set in Scott's Hotel.

G

GAY/LESBIAN

There's not a massive scene in Mallorca and most of it is concentrated in Palma, but citizens are generally gay/lesbian-friendly, and you won't encounter any problems. www.benamics.com is a good 'what's on' site, and there are quite a few lively clubs and bars in the old town.

GREEN ISSUES

Mallorca has invested heavily in developing 'slow tourism' by expanding hiking trails, bicycle routes and *agroturismos* (rural hotels and restaurants) which often grow their own produce.

HEALTH

Inoculations
None required.

Health care and insurance
EU citizens are eligible for free treatment in state-run hospitals. UK visitors should obtain a European Health Insurance Card (EHIC) from a post office or online (www.ehic.org.uk). Visitors from the US will need private health insurance, and it is strongly advised that all travellers take out medical and travel insurance.

Pharmacies and hospitals
Major hospitals and clinics in Palma include: **Centro Médico**, Edificio Reina Constanza, Passeig Marítim (Porto Pi) 8; tel: 971 707 035/55 (many of the staff speak English); and the private **Clínica Femenía SA**, Carrer Camilo José Cela 20; tel: 971 452 323, where some staff also speak English and German.

Most towns and villages have first aid stations or doctor's surgeries: the *Casa de Socorro* or *Cruz (Creu) Roja*. There are pharmacies *(farmàcies)* on most main streets in Palma (look out for the green cross), and in all major towns.

HOURS AND HOLIDAYS

Hours still revolve around the long lunchtime siesta, though that is slowly changing. Shop hours are 10am–2pm and 5–8pm. Small museums keep similar hours, but larger ones increasingly stay open all day.

Banks are only open in the mornings from 9am–2pm, Monday to Friday, but some open on Saturday in winter. Restaurants serve lunch from 1.30–3.30pm. In the evening local people usually eat between 9.30–11pm.

INTERNET FACILITIES

Internet cafés abound in Palma, though these are giving way to mobile logging on in bars, cafés and hotels via Wi-fi. Outside the city it's a bit trickier.

LANGUAGE

Mallorca's language is Mallorquí, a dialect of Catalan. During Franco's dictatorship the teaching and publication of Catalan was banned, and replaced by Spanish/Castilian *(Castellano)*, although people still spoke the language at home. With the arrival of regional autonomy in 1978, Catalan/Mallorquí was re-established, and has become a symbol of Mallorcan identity, although everyone also speaks Spanish.

Above from far left: stock up on Mallorca's signature pastries; go green and hire a bicycle for your stay.

As a result of this, maps and street signs use Castilian or Catalan at random. Most words are fairly similar, but some are completely unrelated. Signs indicating various points of touristic or other interest are almost always in Catalan. Throughout this book, we have tried to give the Catalan version of the place name.

English	Castilian	Catalan
Avenue	*Avenida*	*Avinguda*
Baths	*Baños*	*Banys*
Bay	*Bahia*	*Badia*
Beach	*Playa*	*Platja*
Cathedral	*Catedral*	*Seu*
City	*Ciudad*	*Ciutat*
City Hall	*Ayunta-miento*	*Ajunta-ment*
Caves	*Cuevas*	*Coves*
Mountain	*Monte*	*Puig*
Museum	*Museo*	*Museu*
Palace	*Palacio*	*Palau*
Park	*Parque*	*Parc*
Quay	*Muelle*	*Moll*
Square	*Plaza*	*Plaça*
Street	*Calle*	*Carrer*
Theatre	*Teatro*	*Teatre*
Village	*Pueblo*	*Pobla*
Welcome	*Bienvenido*	*Benvinguts*

Place names and street names

Castilian	Catalan
La Llonja	*Sa Llotja*
La Granja	*Sa Granja*
Avenida Jaime III	*Avinguda Jaume III*
San Elmo	*Sant Elm*
La Puebla	*Sa Pobla*
San Juan	*Sant Joan*

LOST PROPERTY

There are lost property departments at the airport on the ground floor (tel: 971 789 456) and at Palma's Town Hall. It is also worth checking with the police station nearest to where you lost your belongings.

M

MAPS

Free tourist maps of Palma are given out at most hotels and the tourist office, likewise in bigger towns like Sóller. In rural areas maps are useful for getting your bearings, but not very reliable for route planning. La Casa de la Mapa, Carrer Sant Domingo 13, Palma, sells detailed maps.

MEDIA

Print media

Most UK and German papers arrive daily in Palma and the main resorts, along with the *International Herald Tribune, Wall Street Journal* and *USA Today*. The English-language *Majorca Daily Bulletin* gives local and UK news and entertainment listings. Local publications the *Diario de Mallorca* and *Guía del Ocio* (www.guiadelocio.com/illes-balears) are good for up-to-the-minute information on what's on, and all the Spanish national newspapers and magazines are widely available.

Above:
lunch alfresco in
Palma.

Radio

The BBC World Service and Voice of America (the latter on shortwave only) can be received on any good radio. The Palma local radio station broadcasts in English 24 hours a day on 103.2 FM.

Television

Most hotels and bars have television, broadcasting in Castilian, Catalan and Mallorquí. All but the smallest of hotels generally have satellite channels (predominantly German, but also French, channels along with the ubiquitous English-language Sky, BBC, CNN, etc.).

MONEY

Currency

The euro has been the Spanish monetary unit since 2002.

Credit cards

Major international credit cards Visa, Eurocard and MasterCard are widely accepted, but smaller businesses tend to prefer cash. American Express is only accepted in some places.

Cash machines

Credit and debit cards are useful for obtaining cash from ATMs – cash machines – found in all towns and resorts; they usually offer the best exchange rate, though many banks charge commission. Many travel agencies exchange foreign currency, and *casas de cambio* stay open outside banking hours.

Tipping

In some restaurants service is already included (look for *servicio incluído* on the bill). Otherwise, tips range from rounding up to the nearest euro at a bar, to 10 percent in a smart restaurant.

Taxes

Spain applies a standard rate of VAT (IVA) of 18 percent on most goods and services, including hotels; 8 percent is charged on foodstuffs and in restaurants.

P

POLICE

In an emergency dial 112.

There are three types of police, distinguishable by their uniforms: in black and white are the Policía Nacional, who are in charge of most things. The Policía Municipal (Local or Metropolitan) are responsible for traffic control while the Guardia Civil, still dressed in traditional dark-green uniforms, have jurisdiction only in rural areas.

POST

Palma's main post office is at Carrer Constitució 5 and is open Monday to Friday 9am–2pm, 5–8pm, Saturday 9am–1pm. Other post offices on the island (all recognisable by a yellow and white sign and the words *Correos y Telégrafos*) are only open 9am–2pm. Post boxes are yellow.

Stamps can also be bought at tobacconists *(estancos)*, which are easily

identifiable by their maroon and yellow *Tabacos* sign over the door. A postcard or letter to countries in Europe currently costs 62 cents (€0.62), to the US 78 cents (€0.78).

PUBLIC HOLIDAYS

As in all Catholic countries, local saints' days may be celebrated as holidays, but only the days of the major saints *(see the list below)* are public holidays throughout the island.

1 Jan: New Year's Day (Año Nuevo/ Any Nou)
6 Jan: Epiphany (Reyes Magos/Reis Mags)
19 Mar: St Joseph (San José/Sant Josep)
Good Friday (Viernes Santo/Divendres Sant)
1 May: Labour Day (Dia del Trabajo/ Treball)
Ninth Thursday after Easter: Corpus Christi
24 June: St John (San Juan/Sant Joan)
29 June: St Peter and Paul (San Pedro y San Pablo/Sant Pere i Sant Pau)
25 July: St James (Santiago/Sant Jaume)
15 Aug: Day of the Assumption (Asunción/Assumpció)
12 Oct: Spanish National Day (Dia de la Hispanidad/Hispanitat)
1 Nov: All Saints (Todos los Santos/ Tots Sants)
6 Dec: Constitution Day (Dia de la Constitución/Constitució)
8 Dec: Immaculate Conception (Inmaculada Concepión/Concepció)
Christmas Day (Navidad/Nadal)

R

RELIGION

The official religion of Mallorca is Catholicism, though the majority of locals are fairly lax about it. Many attend mass at Christmas and Easter, when it can be quite festive.

S

SMOKING

As of 1 January 2011 smoking has been banned in public places across Spain. Many places provide somewhere to smoke outside, even if it's just an upturned barrel with an ashtray, but be aware that it's becoming increasingly unpopular.

T

TELEPHONES

Public telephone booths are becoming increasingly rare as more and more people have mobile phones; those that do exist still use both coins and cards; international telephone credit cards can also be used. Instructions for use are given in several languages in the

Above:
quad bikes for hire
in Magaluf.

booths. You can also make calls at public telephone offices called *locutorios* – much quieter than making a call on the street, and generally cheaper.

The international code for Spain is 34. To call within Spain, you must always dial the area code (971 for the Balearics), then the number, even when phoning within the same town.

Mobile (cell) phones

Most UK mobile phones can be used in the Balearics, but both making and receiving calls is expensive. Contact your service provider if you are unsure. Renting a phone hasn't really caught on here, but you can buy a pay-as-you-go SIM card from almost any provider: yoigo is one of the cheapest.

TIME ZONES

Spain is on Central European Time, one hour ahead of Greenwich Mean Time. When it is noon in London, it is 1pm in Mallorca.

TOILETS

Toilets *(serveis/servicios)* are generally clean and well kept, but public toilets are few and far between. If you duck into a bar you should buy something – even if it's just a small bottle of water – as most are for patrons only. In Palma, head for a department store such as Els Corte Inglés. *Dones/damas* stands for ladies, *cavallers/caballeros* for gentlemen.

TOURIST INFORMATION

Tourist information is readily available in most parts of Mallorca, although many offices close in winter. The following list is not comprehensive.

Local tourist offices

Palma: Plaça de la Reina 2, tel: 971 712 216; Carrer Constitució 1, tel: 971 725 396; Plaça de Espanya, tel: 971 754 329; Carrer Sant Domingo 11, tel: 971 724 090 (information on Palma only).

Airport: tel: 971 789 556.

Colònia Sant Jordi: Dr Barraquer, tel: 971 656 073 (closed Nov–Mar).

Pollença: Carrer Sant Domingo, tel: 971 535 077.

Port d'Alcúdia: Carrer Mariners s/n, tel: 971 547 257 (closed Nov–Mar).

Port de Pollença: Carrer Joan XXIII 46, tel: 971 865 467.

Port de Sóller: Canonge Oliver 10, tel: 971 633 042 (closed Nov–Mar).

Sóller: Plaça Constitució, tel: 971 630 200.

Valldemossa: Avinguda Arxiduc Lluis Salvador, tel: 971 612 106 (closed Nov–Mar).

TRANSPORT

Airports and arrival

Palma de Mallorca's huge **Son Sant Joan airport** (PMI) is linked by regular scheduled non-stop flights from London, Dublin, Berlin and Frankfurt, with frequent flights from

many other European cities. Flights from the US and Canada also go via London airports and Barcelona or Madrid. Numerous budget airlines fly to Palma from airports all over the UK. Booking via the internet is usually cheapest for flight-only tickets.

The airport is about 11km (7 miles) from the city centre. There are buses every 20 minutes (journey time about 30 minutes). Taxis are readily available (journey time about 15–20 minutes) and fares are reasonable.

Arriving by boat

Car ferries operate daily from Barcelona and Valencia to Palma. The slower, overnight trip takes 8 hours on Trasmediterránea (Moll de Paraires, Estació Marítim 2; tel: 902 454 645 or 971 702 300/971 366 050 in Palma; www.trasmediterranea.com); during peak holiday season, it also operates a faster ferry, which takes 4½ hours. Baleària operates a fast ferry from Barcelona to Alcúdia on Saturday and Sunday, which takes 3½ hours (tel: 902 160 180; www.balearia.net).

Public transport
Buses

There are several bus companies in Mallorca, travelling to virtually every point on the island. In Palma, most services begin at the Plaça de Espanya or the new bus station close by in Carrer Eusebio Estada (near the railway station). City buses are also efficient.

There is a set fare for city journeys, and you buy your ticket on the bus. A Palma bus schedule detailing city routes, from Empresa Municipal de Transports (EMT), is available from the tourist office. Bus services are reduced on Sunday and holidays. Fewer services run during the winter months.

Trains

As well as the famous old train, which runs six times a day (seven on Sunday) between Palma and Sóller, there is a train from Palma's Plaça de Espanya to Inca which runs on to Llubi, Muro and Sa Pobla. Primarily a commuter train, it leaves both the island capital and Inca about once every hour, with extra trains at rush hours, stopping at Santa Maria, Consell and Binissalem along the way. For Sóller trains, tel: 971 752 051; for Inca trains, tel: 971 752 245, or ask at the station.

Taxis

Palma has several taxi ranks, and cabs can be hailed on the street. All have meters and are reasonably priced, though you pay extra for luggage and trips to and from the airport. Trips across the island, however, are quite expensive. Official prices are posted at cab ranks, and drivers also carry a list.

Driving in Mallorca
Rules and regulations

Drive on the right. Seat belts are compulsory for front and back seats. Children under 10 must travel in the back. Don't drink and drive: the per-

mitted blood-alcohol level is low and penalties are strict.

Road conditions

Generally good, although many are narrow, and mountain routes have numerous hairpin bends and can get very busy in the summer. The motorway that loops around to the north of Palma (connecting the airport with points west of the city), is known as the *Via Cintura* and is signposted as such.

Speed limits

Motorways 110kmph (68mph), two-lane highways 100kmph (60mph), other main roads 90kmph (56mph), built-up areas 50kmph (32mph), unless otherwise indicated

Parking

In Palma this can be difficult. Your best bet is to head for one of the city centre underground car parks (for instance at the Plaça Mayor or opposite the cathedral at the Parc de la Mar). Parking fines are steep, and as it is more difficult to collect fines from tourists, there is a tendency to tow away hire cars.

Car hire

This is relatively inexpensive, and all the major international agencies are represented, along with some local agents that are generally cheaper. In high season, book well in advance and remember that local companies often set a minimum rental of three or four days. Always check what's included: third-party insurance is, by law, but fully comprehensive is usually extra and it is advisable to have it. You need to be 21 to hire a car and must have a full driving licence and a credit card.

V

VISAS AND PASSPORTS

British citizens just need a valid passport. Visitors from other EU countries require a valid national identity card. US citizens, Australians and New Zealanders require a valid passport and are automatically authorised for a three-month stay.

W

WEBSITES

Useful websites are peppered throughout the book, but the following are good for general information: www.seemallorca.com: for tips on what's on and where to go. www.mallorca.co.uk: for villa rentals. www.illesbalears.es/ing/majorca: the official tourism portal for the island.

WEIGHTS AND MEASURES

Mallorca uses the metric system.

WOMEN

Women travelling alone will find Mallorca an easy-going, non-threatening place to explore. As anywhere, avoid walking home late at night alone.

Above:
crystal-clear water made for boating; hiring a car is a good option for exploring the island's hinterland.

Mallorca has a wide range of accommodation, ranging from trendy boutiques in Palma to chic farmhouse accommodation inland. Most de luxe accommodation is clustered around the west coast, while you can get great package deals if you head east. This list only covers areas included in the tours, and some areas are stronger than others in terms of places to stay. The Bay of Alcúdia, for example, caters mainly for package tourists, so we recommend staying in nearby Pollença.

The following guide indicates prices for a standard double room in high season, but should be used as an approximate guide only. VAT (IVA) at 8 percent and breakfast are sometimes included in a quoted rate, but it is wise to check.

Palma

Hostal Ritzi

Carrer Apuntadors 6; tel: 971 714 610; www.hostalritzi.com; €

One of Palma's few budget options, the Ritzi occupies an attractive old townhouse just off the lively Passeig de Born. It has 17 rooms, ranging from en suite doubles to bunk-bed dorms

Price for a double room for one night without breakfast:	
€€€€	over 240 euros
€€€	120–240 euros
€€	75–120 euros
€	below 75 euros

for friends sharing. Bonuses are a pleasant courtyard and free Wi-fi in communal areas.

Hotel Bon Sol

Passeig de Illetes 30; tel: 971 402 111; www.hotelbonsol.es; €€€

This quirky family-run hotel is a delight, about a 20-minute taxi ride from the centre. Heavy Spanish furnishings in the lobby are complemented by light, airy bedrooms; gardens and terraces cascade down to the sea, and there's a private beach. Yoga classes and spa facilities are included in the price.

Hotel Born

Carrer Sant Jaume 3, Palma; tel: 971 712 942; www.hotelborn. com; €€

A taste of the Palma that was, this lovingly renovated palace is right in the heart of the city and oozes atmosphere, though some rooms are showing their age. Regardless, it's spotlessly clean and the open-air courtyard where breakfast is served is hard to beat.

Hotel Feliz

Avinguda de Joan Miró 74; tel: 971 288 847; www.hotelfeliz.com; €€€

One of the grooviest newcomers to arrive on the scene for a while, Feliz has a Scandinavian aesthetic boosted by lots of bright colour woven into an old 1960s apartment block. The 'fish tank' swimming pool on the terrace is fun, while the ample lounge stuffed

with squishy sofas is a great place to chill out at night.

Portixol

Carrer Sirena 27, Portixol; tel: 971 271 800; www.portixol.com; €€€

The hotel of choice for hip young things wanting to hang out on the beach, Portixol ticks a lot of boxes: sexy lounge and cocktail bar, great food, a pool to be seen in, plentiful pampering treatments. The seafaring theme in the bedrooms extends to binoculars for watching the wildlife.

Puro

Carrer Montenegro 12, Palma; tel: 971 425 450; www.purohotel.com; €€€€

Arguably the city's trendiest hotel, Puro has designer chic emanating from every faux animal skin-covered pouf or sleek leather armchair. It pays to be a creature of the night when staying here – it's somewhere to party rather than chill out; also has a tasteful beach club just beyond Ciutat Jardi.

Tres

Carrer Apuntadors 3; tel: 971 717 333; www.hoteltres.com; €€€

A sleek, contemporary renovation of an aristocratic townhouse, Tres attracts a more grown-up crowd than Puro, without being stuffy. Rooms are stylish and spacious, the central courtyard and lounge are both great places for breakfast and hanging out, and two roof terraces give splendid city views.

Hotel Rural Nord

Plaça d'es Triquet 4, Estellencs; tel: 971 149 006; www.hotelruralnord.com; €€

This traditional stone village house is built around a courtyard that has been revamped with a designer's touch. Sunny bedrooms, local produce and a restored olive mill for drinks at the end of the day deliver far more than you would expect from the price tag. A real bargain.

Mar-i-Vent

Carrer Major 49, Banyalbufar; tel: 971 618 000; www.hotelmarivent.com; €€€

This family-run hotel is one of the original hotels to spring up on the west coast. The bedrooms are light and airy if fairly basic, but the main reason to stay here is to take advantage of its extraordinary clifftop pool and dazzling sea views. Closed Dec–Jan.

Villages of the Tramuntana

L'Hermitage

Tel: 971 180 303; www.hermitage-hotel.com; €€€–€€€€

One of the most secluded and most exclusive hotels on the island, yet more affordable than its more famous counterparts (like La Residencia), this is a great escape for discerning travellers. Gorgeous gardens and terraces, capa-

Above:
Hotel Bon Sol's opulent lobby.

cious rooms with four-poster beds, excellent food and a de luxe spa elevate it to something really special.

Son Palou

Plaça de la Església s/n, Orient; tel: 971 148 282; www.sonpalou. com; €€

Tranquil, beautiful and stylish, Son Palou is regularly voted best base on the island by hikers, so book well in advance if you want to stay here. It has cosy lounges (complete with crackling fires in winter), romantic bedrooms, rambling gardens, huge pool and a superb restaurant specialising in traditional country cooking.

Valldemossa to Lluc

Es Molí

Carretera Valldemossa–Deià s/n; tel: 971 639 090; www.esmoli.com; €€€€

Recently under new management, Es Molí is a magical place occupying several acres of lush gardens at the foot of Es Teix mountain, overlooking the sea. A recent refurbishment has given it a more contemporary appeal, but the personal service and romantic ambience remain unchanged. Access to a private beach – Sa Muleta – is an added bonus. Closed Nov–mid-Apr.

Fonda Villa Verde

Carrer Ramón Llull 19, Deià; tel: 971 639 037; €

In a quiet backstreet right in the heart of the village of Deià, this simple hostal

Price for a double room for one night without breakfast:	
€€€€	over 240 euros
€€€	120–240 euros
€€	75–120 euros
€	below 75 euros

is perfect for those looking to explore the region without blowing the budget. Rooms are basic and fairly chintzy (lace curtains, doilies), but it has a lovely patio for sitting out and revelling in the peace and quiet. Closed Dec–Feb.

La Residencia

Son Moragues, Deià; tel: 971 639 011; www.hotel-laresidencia.com; €€€€

Probably Mallorca's most famous hotel, La Residencia is loved by visiting celebrities and European glitterati. Set in two chic and elegant 16th-century manor houses, this is the place to be if you value privacy and a hotel capable of satisfying your every whim. The modern Mallorcan restaurant El Olivo is one of the best in Spain.

S'Hotel d'es Puig

Es Puig 4, Deià; tel: 971 639 409; www.hoteldespuig.com; €€

A fantastic option of the chic and cheap variety, this small village hotel has sleek, contemporary rooms, a pool and flagstone terrace, fabulous views and friendly, family service. It has also

had a host of illustrious guests over the years (Robert Graves used to put his pals here) and retains a bohemian atmosphere. Closed mid-Nov–Feb.

Sóller and Port de Sóller

Es Port

Carrer Antonio Montis s/n, Port de Sóller; tel: 971 631 650; www.hotel esport.com; €€

This meticulously restored 17th-century stone farmhouse is hugely popular with hikers. With several living rooms built around an ancient olive press, rambling gardens, two huge pools (outdoor and in) and crackling fires in the winter, you can see why so many people keep coming back for more.

Hotel Esplendido

Es Traves s/n, Port de Sóller; tel: 971 631 850; www.portixol.nu/esplendido; €€€

The grooviest hotel on the seafront, Esplendido is owned by the same people as the Portixol in Palma and despite its size has a boutique appeal. It reopened in the spring of 2011 after a major revamp and the addition of a spa, firmly establishing itself as the place *du jour* among style-savvy travellers.

L'Avenida

Gran Via 9, Sóller; tel: 971 634 075; www.avenida-hotel.com; €€€

One of the hippest boutiques on the island, L'Avenida has just eight luxury suites, each more glamorous than the next. Elsewhere, communal areas are dripping in luxury, while the arcaded terraces around the pool are the height of sophisticated elegance. This place offers a real treat and is a fantastic choice for romantic weekend getaways.

Pollença and Fortmentor

Hotel Formentor

Platja de Formentor s/n, Formentor; tel: 971 899 100; www.hotelformentor.net; €€€€

Overlooking the beach, this classic hotel has been around since the 1950s, when it was something of a haven for travelling stars; Ava Gardener and Liz Taylor have both stayed here. These days it attracts business and leisure travellers for its spot on one of the most beautiful beaches on the island.

L'Hostal Pollença

Carrer Mercat 18, Pollença; tel: 971 535 282; www.pollensahotels.com; €€

This place is excellent value for money: it's really a B&B that's gone upmarket, with a lively ambience, colourful rooms all with en suite bathrooms, and a groovy retro public room for trading books and gossiping. Breakfast is served at the sister-hotel around the corner, the Hotel Juma on the main square.

Above: the luxurious La Residencia has a wonderful setting in Deià.

Son Brull

Carretera Palma–Pollenfa Km 49.8, Pollença; tel: 971 535 353; €€€

One of the most stylish boutiques on the island, Son Brull is a monastery that has been converted into a shrine to contemporary minimalism. Perfect for design aficionados, yet unexpectedly welcoming to children; expect lots of clean lines, futuristic food and impeccable service.

Artà and Cala Torta

Bar Restaurante Sa Duaia

Carretera Artà–Cala Torta Km 8; tel: 651 826 416; €€

A secret hideaway on the bluff above Artà, this place attracts an alternative crowd who enjoy a bit of splendid isolation. Apartments are rustic but comfortable, it has a great pool, and though the food is fairly ordinary, the wildness of the terrace makes it one of the best on the island.

Cala Sant Vicenç

Carrer Maressers 2, Cala Sant Vicenç; tel: 971 530 250; www. hotelcala.com; €€€

Tucked away in the woods, this seaside

Price for a double room for one night without breakfast:

€€€€	over 240 euros
€€€	120–240 euros
€€	75–120 euros
€	below 75 euros

hotel has a heated outdoor pool, sauna and lovely gardens, as well as a highly recommended restaurant, the Cavall Bernat. It is starting to show its age a bit, but with the beach just a short stroll away, it is wonderful for young families. Closed Dec–Jan.

Cases de Son Barbassa

Carretera Cala Mesquida s/n, Capdepera; tel: 971 565 776; www. sonbarbassa.com; €€€

This chic rural retreat is like the new-wave *agroturismos* of Ibiza: a collection of spacious suites built of stone and wood spread across several olive groves, a pool area surrounded by draped day beds, fantastic food and the sensation that you're miles from anywhere.

Hotel Casal d'Artà

Carrer Rafael Blanes 19, Artà; tel: 971 829 163; www.casaldarta.de; €

A good budget option, this friendly townhouse at the top of town is a delight. Typical island decor goes well with a laid-back vibe, while a sunny dining room and terrace make breakfast a time to linger. The roof is a wonderful place to end the day with a glass of wine.

Caves and Grottoes of the East

Can Simoneta

Carretera Artà–Canyamel Km 8, Capdepera; tel: 971 81 61 10; www. cansimoneta.com; €€€

A spectacularly located boutique hotel, occupying several acres of cliff-top above the sea. Inside, think cool minimalism, outside manicured lawns, hammocks and a staircase to a private beach. With just six rooms, service is highly personalised – perfect for a romantic getaway or honeymoon.

Cap Vermell

Plaça es Pins de Ses Vegues 1, Canyamel, Capdepera; tel: 971 841 157; www.grupocapvermell.com; €€

This 1970s-style block on the edge of the sea has a certain Americana retro appeal, with acres of glass and a bleached-wood dining and lounge area. Rooms are more basic, but the terrace is fantastic (as is the food), and it's not a bad little beach spot for the price.

Es Trenc and the South

Hostal Colonial

Ingeniero Gabriel Roca 9, Colònia de Sant Jordi; tel: 971 655 278; €

A basic but pleasing little place in a quiet fishing village, this *hostal* is big on family seaside appeal, with its own ice-cream parlour and a huge range of hot chocolate. It's also one of the cheapest places to stay on the island.

S'Hotelet de Santanyí

Plaça Major 23, Santanyí; tel: 971 653 585; www.hoteletsantanyi.com; €€€

This smartly renovated townhouse is a welcome addition to Santanyí's hip village scene. Crisp white linen sheets

against honey-coloured stone make for soothing weekends away, while the lively central plaza location gives a sense of being at the heart of things.

Felanitx to Petra

Es Reco de Randa

Carrer Font 21, Randa; tel: 971 660 997; www.esrecoderanda.com; €€

This is a sweet country hotel with old-fashioned rooms and plenty of soul. It's a pleasant base if you want to get off the beaten path a little, and features some nice extras like live music and paella nights through the summer.

Wine Country

Reads

Carretera Santa Maria–Alaro s/n, Santa Maria del Camí; tel: 971 140 261; www.readshotel.com; €€€€

This glorious stately home is family-run and right by the wineries. If that's not your thing, they offer plenty of other activities including one of the finest spas on the island, professional cycling facilities and top-notch food.

Scott's

Plaça de la Església 12, Binissalem; tel: 971 870 100; €€€

An elegantly comfortable hotel in quiet Binissalem, well located for wine-tasting and exploring the central plains. Period furniture gives it a cosy air, while pleasant courtyards are great for relaxing at the end of the day. Service is personal and friendly. Early booking is essential.

Above from far left: a peaceful room at Can Simoneta; looking out over Artà; the wonderful terrace at Cap Vermell.

When it comes to eating out in Mallorca there's plenty of diversity, though certain areas are much stronger than others. As in most cities, Palma has something to suit a range of tastes and budgets, but once you get outside urban areas it helps to know what you are doing. The restaurants selected follow, roughly, the routes outlined in the walks and tours, but in some cases it's worth travelling a bit further to eat well. You eat much better on the southeast coast than the northeast, and it is worth making the detour if food is the main purpose of your trip.

Opening hours, especially in rural areas and depending on the season, can be a bit erratic. If you want to be sure, it pays to call in advance.

Eating out is no longer particularly cheap, though there are some bargains to be had, and these have been highlighted as much as possible.

Palma

Bon Lloc

Carrer Sant Feliu 7; tel: 971 718 617; L only; €

This vegetarian restaurant has been around since the 1970s, and continues to draw a crowd for its set-price lunch menu. The food is inventive and healthy, ranging from wholemeal bread with home-made soups to more substantial pasta and bean dishes. The atmosphere is convivial thanks to lots of longstanding regulars.

El Bungalow

Carrer Esculls 2, Ciutat Jardí; tel: 971 262 738; L, D; €€€

Ask any chef in Mallorca their favourite fish restaurant and at least half of them will come back with this place. Little more than a stone shack on the beach, it serves fish just the way it should be: fresh and simply grilled – and it's just 15 minutes from central Palma.

Es Parlament

Carrer Conquistador 11; tel: 971 726 026; www.restaurantparlament.com; Mon–Sat L, D; €€€

With its glittering chandeliers, wood-panelled walls and generally aristocratic air, this Art Nouveau gem is somewhere to don your fancy clothes and go all out for a treat. It's posh, but accessibly so, and serves excellent gourmet Mallorcan cuisine.

Fábrica 23

Carrer Cotoner 42–44; tel: 971 453 125; www.fabrica23.com; Tue–Fri L, D, Sat D, Sun L; €€€

In the increasingly trendy Santa Catalina area, this hip little eatery serves quality Mediterranean cuisine in a lively atmosphere. Daily specials are chalked up on the blackboard, the *menú del día* costs €12, and it's one of the best places in town for a juicy Argentinian steak.

La Bóveda

Passeig Sagrera 3; tel: 971 714 863; L, D; €

This iconic Palma tapas bar is the place to go to rub shoulders with local people and tuck into plates of maple-sweet *jamón Ibérico*, slabs of Manchego cheese, *pimientos de padrón* (sweet, and occasionally spicy fried green peppers) and heaps of local seafood. Sit at the bar, or on the terrace and enjoy with an ice-cold *caña* (small draught beer) or a glass of the local wine.

Simply Fosh

Carrer Missió 7a; tel: 971 720 114; www.simplyfosh.com; L, D; €€€€

Marc Fosh is one of Mallorca's most brilliant chefs. A staunch proponent of local produce, his fresh take on tra-ditional recipes like rice with *sobrasada* (the local pork sausage generously laced with paprika) ensure intensely satisfying eating, and his flagship restaurant is just the place to try it. For a taste of Fosh on a budget go for the bargain lunch (€19), or check one of his other two branches: Blanquerna de la Taberna (Carrer Blan-querna 6; tel: 971 290 108) for sit-down tapas, and Misa Braserie (Can Macanet 1a; tel: 971 595 301) for modern Mal-lorcan bistro-style fare.

> Price for a two-course meal for one with a glass of house wine:
>
> €€€€ = over €40
> €€€ = €25–€40
> €€ = €15–€25
> € = below €15

Illeta

Avinguda de la Platja 1, Camp de Mar; tel: 971 235 025; L, D; €€€

Camp de Mar is a massively popular resort, and arriving here for lunch isn't immediately auspicious. How-ever, in the middle of the sheltered bay is an islet with this restaurant serving boat-fresh seafood. It is accessed by a wooden bridge and is as good a place as any along this stretch to stop for a dip.

Limón y Chelo

Asociación Cultural Sa Taronja, Carrer Andalucía 23, Andratx; tel: 971 136 368; L, D; €€

Something of a well-kept secret, this place works for all seasons. Lushly planted gardens are magical in the summer, while the cosy, fire-lit dining room is a boon in winter months. Live music is staged throughout the year, along with wine-tastings and other cultural events, and the food is superb, much of it home-grown and organic.

Son Tomás

Carrer Baronia, 17, Banyalbufar; tel: 971 618 149; L, D; €€

This region isn't particularly strong when it comes to dining, but Son Tomás has enjoyed a sterling reputa-tion since the mid-1980s for sturdy Mediterranean cooking. It buzzes with atmosphere, and the fish soup, paellas and *fideus* are all firm favourites.

Above:
Simply Fosh is one of Palma's standout restaurants.

Villages of the Tramuntana

Ca Na Toneta

Carrer Horitzó 21, Caimari; tel: 971 515 226; L, D; €€–€€€

Like a little dolls' house, Ca Na Toneta and its creators, Maria and Teresa Solivellas, ooze charm. The delightful dining room makes a fitting backdrop for dishes of organic products they grow themselves. They serve only a six-course tasting menu, which changes weekly to reflect the nuances of the seasons. It's one worth travelling for.

Dalt Muntanya

Carretera Bunyola–Orient Km 10; tel: 971 615 373; www.daltmuntanya. net; L, D; €€€

Part of a hotel of the same name, this restaurant has a fabulous terrace from which to take in the scenery over a hale and hearty menu of hikers' favourites. Plenty of vegetable-rich starters, but the stars are slowly roasted leg of lamb or suckling pig: both superb.

Mandala

Carrer Nueva 1, Orient; tel: 971 615 285; L, D; €€€

This romantic, cottage-style spot combines the best Mallorcan ingredients with flavours from Asia to great effect, and is an unusual find here in the mountains. Popular in the cooler months when people are spending several days exploring local trails, dishes range from duck breast with plums to fish curries and spicy puddings.

Traffic at Can Xim

Plaça de la Vila 8, Alaró; tel: 971 879 117; L, D; €€€

Despite the unlikely-sounding name, this is a charmer, with its ancient wood beams and rustic decor – just the sort of place to hole up for a long, lazy winter lunch. The food tends to the heavy, but features tasty combinations like monkfish and eggplant, and stewed rabbit with confit onions.

Valldemossa to Lluc

El Olivo

Carrer Son Canals s/n, Deià; tel: 971 639 011, www.hotel-laresiden cia-com; L, D; €€€€

La Residencia's fine dining restaurant draws legions of fans who can't afford a night at the hotel, but can treat themselves to a taste of the high life in elegant and refined surroundings. The modern Mallorcan tasting menu changes seasonally and is one of the best on the island.

El Barrigon

Carrer Archiduque Luis Salvador 19; tel: 971 639 139; www.xelini.com; Tue–Sun 12.30pm–1am, L, D; closed 10 Nov–27 Dec; €€

One of the more low-key eateries in Deià, this lively little tapas bar on a pretty terrace has been going strong for 24 years and draws locals and visitors alike for its unfussy fare. Try the smoked ham, aubergines stuffed with goat's cheese and their speciality of

mar i muntanya (chicken and prawns). Live jazz sessions are hosted on Saturdays through the winter.

Sa Fonda de Lluc

Plaça dels Peregrins 1, Lluc; tel: 971 871 525; www.lluc.net; L, D; €€
This vast dining room of austere stone columns and flagstones was the pilgrims' canteen, and it has a certain monastic austerity. It's a good place for dinner at the end of a long day, to enjoy their speciality – wild mountain goat with jugs of lusty red wine. Just decide in advance who is going to drive home.

Sebastián

Carrer Felipe Bauzá s/n, Deià; tel: 971 639 417; L, D; €€€
An excellent choice for a special night out if your budget doesn't quite reach the dizzying heights of El Olivo. The warm, candlelit ambience and cleverly constructed dishes, such as slow-baked lamb with honey, are just right for a romantic evening.

Sóller and
Port of Sóller

Lua

Carrer Santa Catalina 1, Port de Sóller; tel: 971 634 745; L, D; €€
A pretty little restaurant in the Santa Caterina fishermen's district, with a more inventive take on the region's fish produce than most. Spread over two floors, the nicest place to sit is on the narrow terrace with views over the port, while tucking into local orange salad followed by a succulent fillet of John Dory slathered with *salsa verde*.

Sa Teulera

Carretera Lluc–Pollença s/n, Sóller; tel: 971 631 111; L only; €€
A classic for Sunday lunch, it's worth the drive (or uphill hike) from town. Roast meats cooked over almond shells are the order of the day. It gets packed to the gills, so book in advance and reserve a place on the terrace if the weather is good – it has spectacular views.

Pollença and Formentor

Ca'n Costa

Carrer Costa and Carrer Llobera 11; tel: 971 531 276; Mon–Sat D; closed mid Nov–start March; €€€
Housed in Pollença's first cinema, this regal-looking restaurant is perfect for romantic dinners, offering two lounge areas for a pre- and post-dinner drinks as well as pretty outdoor dining. Chef William Kaberry's modern Mediterranean cuisine doesn't disappoint

Above from far left:
exquisitely presented fish at Simply Fosh *(see p.101)*; mood lighting at El Olivo.

> Price for a two-course meal for one with a glass of house wine:
>
> €€€€ = over €40
> €€€ = €25–€40
> €€ = €15–€25
> € = below €15

either. Try grilled scallops drizzled with vodka and lemon, succulent rosemary monkfish skewers and roast cod fillet on saffron-scented mussels, and feather-light white and dark chocolate fondant to finish.

Il Giardino

Plaça Major 11, Pollença; tel: 971 534 302; Br, L, D; €€

A family-run trattoria on the square, a great place to sit and watch the world go by at night, when it's at its most convivial. Wood-fire cooked pizzas and home-made pastas are excellent.

Artà and Cala Torta

Finca Es Serral

Carretera Cala Torta Km 5, Artà; tel: 971 835 336; L, D; €€

It's a delight to know that restaurants like this still exist: Es Serral is the very heart and soul of a true farm restaurant. All the fruit and vegetables are grown on the owner's plot, the meat reared locally and the food home-cooked. Reserve well in advance to secure a table (and opening hours can be erratic, especially out of season), but it is well worth the forward planning.

Caves and Grottoes of the East

Es Clos

Carrer Convento 17, Alqueria Blanca; tel: 971 653 404; L, D; €€€€

Finding an upmarket restaurant in the middle of a tiny little village in the back of beyond is fairly typical for Mallorca, hence the need to keep on exploring. Es Clos serves wonderfully decadent modern Mallorquín dishes such as ravioli and truffle sauce, slowly braised Mallorcan rabbit on couscous, and elderberry mousse.

Florian

Carrer Cristófal Colom 5, Porto Colom; tel: 971 824 171; L, D; €€€

Porto Colom has several good fish and seafood places clustered around the shore. Florian is one of the trendier ones: the chef places his cooking style firmly in the new wave, serving dishes like shellfish and fennel couscous and lobster with vanilla.

La Bodeguita

Avinguda América 14, Cala Ratjada; tel: 971 819 062; L, D; €

La Bodeguita does bargain-priced tapas and hearty main courses. Expect fairly basic service and food that is filling rather than award-winning, but it has pretty views over the front and is good for something cheap and cheerful.

Price for a two-course meal for one with a glass of house wine:

€€€€ = over €40
€€€ = €25–€40
€€ = €15–€25
€ = below €15

La Llotja

Carrer Pescadores s/n, Porto Colom; tel: 971 825 165; L, D; €€€

A smart fish restaurant in the port of this little town, La Llotja is raised up above the beach on a glassed-in first floor. It has fantastic views, which can be especially dramatic in stormy weather – it's open year-round – and offers a solid repertoire of locally caught, simply cooked fish and seafood.

Es Trenc and the South

Asador Es Teatre

Plaça San Bartolomé 4, Ses Salines; L, D; tel: 971 649 540; €€

One of the trendiest restaurants in the south, this atmospheric Argentinian steak house covers two floors (one of the them a wrap-around gallery) and specialises in *criollo*-style barbecue (where the meat is spatch-cocked and placed around the flame as opposed to on it).

Restaurante Sa Llotja

Port de Colònia de Sant Jordi s/n Colònia de Sant Jordi; L, D; tel: 971 656 555; €€€

Sa Llotja is situated right in the middle of the spruced-up port area of this largely untouched little town, and the fish and seafood comes in straight off the boats in the harbour. Portions are huge.

Felanitx to Petra

Es Brot

Carrer Ràpita 44, Campos; tel: 971 160 263; L, D; €€€

Often described as the best traditional restaurant in Mallorca, Es Brot's diverse menu of classics like pork-stuffed cabbage leaves, pickled partridge and sturdy rice dishes are excellent. Be sure to come with a healthy appetite.

Wine Country

Celler Can Amer

Carrer Pau 39, Inca; tel: 971 501 261; L, D; €€

Opened in 1700, the barrels, copper pots and flagstone floors make this a wonderfully atmospheric place for long, boozy lunches (particularly in the winter). Chef Antonia Cantallops combines the Jewish, Arabic and Christian influences of the island's culinary heritage to create her variation on traditional cuisine, but it's always superb. The shoulder of lamb stuffed with aubergines and *sobrasada* is awe-inspiring.

Celler Can Ripoll

Carrer Jaume Armengol 4, Inca; tel: 971 500 024; www.canripoll.com; B, Br, L, D; €€

Opened in 1768, this cellar restaurant was, like Can Amer, used mainly by local workers as a place to fill their wine jugs. Food wasn't offered until the 1940s, the speciality being a fairly hardcore *frito mallorquín* – stir-fried offal. These days you can also find excellent but rather more pedestrian stuffed cabbage leaves and roast suckling pig.

If you're looking for frenetic nightlife Mallorca probably isn't the island for you, although things can get lively in Palma in the summer. Once outside the city you will find a much slower pace of life, especially when you hit rural areas and some of the quieter coastal towns and villages. If you're staying in Estellencs (tour 4), for example, the most you can hope for is a beer in the village bar, although tourist resorts tend to be livelier. For that reason, the bulk of this section concentrates its attention on what's happening in Palma, with a sprinkling of recommended places elsewhere.

Palma

Ábaco

Carrer Sant Joan 1; tel: 971 714 939; www.bar-abaco.com; free

No visit to Palma is complete without stopping at this legendary cocktail bar. Famed for its over-the-top decor, and gigantic fruit and floral arrangements, there's nowhere quite like it for your gin and tonic.

Abraxas

Passeig Marítim 42; tel: 971 455 908; www.abraxasmallorca.com; charge

This stretch of road that whips around the Bay of Palma is where most of the big clubs are found. Abraxas was formerly known as Pacha, and is dripping in glamour. It's the only place to go for serious clubbing, and the only club in Mallorca to attract the big-name DJs. Dress to impress to stand a hope of getting in.

Auditorium

Passeig Marítim 18; tel: 971 735 328; www.auditoriumdepalma.com; charge

Home to the Ciutat de Palma Symphony Orchestra and a host of cultural events throughout the year, ranging from contemporary dance to opera. Check out what's on ahead of your trip; tickets can be hard to come by.

Jazz Voyeur Club

Carrer Apuntadors 5; no phone; free

Formerly the Barcelona Jazz Club, this was one of the city's first live music venues, and dedicates itself mainly to live jazz and blues, with the odd jam session for good measure.

Made in Brasil

Passeig Marítim 33; tel: 670 372 390; charge

If you seek samba, salsa and other snake-hipped Latin rhythms, this is where to head; the place sizzles until 4am most nights of the week, attracting some serious dancers.

Multicines Renoir

Carrer Emperatrix Eugenia 6; tel: 971 297 301; www.cinesrenoir.com; charge

The only original-language cinema in

town, the Renoir group, with venues across Spain, shows a fair number of independent movies as well as the blockbusters. Auditoriums are small and cosy, giving it an art-house feel.

Puro Beach

Cala Estancia s/n (airport exit), Palma; tel: 971 744 744; www. purobeach.com; charge

The first of a growing number of swanky beach clubs to pepper the coast, Puro is the full-time haunt of the island's beautiful crowd in summer. It opens early for sunbathing by the pool, yoga sessions and champagne brunches, segueing effortlessly into a more clubby vibe once the sun goes down.

Tito's

Passeig Marítim s/n; tel: 971 730 017; www.titosmallorca.com; charge

Tito's attracts a slightly more grown-up crowd than other clubs along the disco mile and is the longest-standing club on the island. It has a certain old-school appeal with an exterior glass lift and laser light show, spectacular views of the port by night and a strong repertoire of favourite club anthems.

Virtual Club

Passeig Illetes 60, Illetes; tel: 971 703 235; www.virtualclub.es; free

Mallorca's second beach club – after Puro – Virtual is a little less achingly trendy and offers a more relaxed vibe.

Like Puro, you can spend the day lounging by the sea, have lunch, then let your sundowner lead you gently into the evening.

Wineing

Carrer Apuntadors 24, Palma; tel: 971 214 011; www.wineing.es; free

This wine bar was ground-breaking in introducing the first serve-yourself pouring system to Spain, and it's a great way to sample several different Mallorcan wines by the glass. There's a lively, yet laid-back atmosphere by night, and they serve decent tapas as an accompaniment.

Outside Palma

Casino

Urbanización Sol de Mallorca, Magaluf, Calvià; tel: 971 130 000 (open until 5am); charge

The island's only casino can be fun. It's a fairly upmarket place once you get away from the slot machines, and provides a good excuse to get dressed up and indulge in an *Ocean's Eleven*-style fantasy.

Pirates

Carretera Sa Porrassa 12, Magaluf; tel: 971 130 411; www.piratesad venture.com; charge

The show at Pirates has been running since the early 1980s and is wildly popular. Book well in advance and treat the whole family to what may be the best '*espectaculo*' this side of Broadway.

Above:
Mallorca has plentiful options for when the sun goes down.

CREDITS

Insight Step by Step Mallorca
Written by: Tara Stevens
Series Editor: Carine Tracanelli
Commissioning Editor: Sarah Sweeney
Map Production: APA Cartography Department
Picture Manager: Steve Lawrence
Art Editor: Ian Spick
Production: Tynan Dean and Linton Donaldson
Photography by: APA: Greg Gladman, except
AKG: 56B; Alamy 38TL, 43; Bodegas Angel:
7BR, 77, 78, 79, 80T; Can Simoneta: 82, 98TL; El
Olivio: 103; Fotolibra 62-63; Grupo Cap Vermell:
99TR; Robert Harding: 7MR, 16TL &TR, 18TL,
23TL, 65, 66, 68, 69, 71, 73B, 81T; Hotel Bon Sol:
95-96; iStockphoto: 14T, 49B, 52, 53, 53B, 57T,
80-81, 81B, 104; Orient Express (La Residenca):
96-97; Parc del Mar 28-29; Photolibrary: 40TL,
41, 59, 60, 70, 71B; Simply Fosh: 100-101, 102;
Superstock: 37T;

The map on p.48 derived from OpenStreetMap
© OpenStreetMap and Contributors, CC-BY-SA

Front cover: main image: 4Corners Images;
bottom left and right: iStockphoto
Back cover: bottom left and right: fotolia

Printed by: CTPS-China

Although Insight Guides and the authors of
this book have taken all reasonable care in pre-
paring it, we make no warranty about the accuracy
or completeness of its content, and, to the max-
imum extent permitted, disclaim all liability
arising from its use.

CONTACTING THE EDITORS

We would appreciate it if readers would alert us to
errors or outdated information by writing to us
at insight@apaguide.co.uk or APA Publications,
PO Box 7910, London SE1 1WE, UK.

www.insightguides.com

DISTRIBUTION

Worldwide
APA Publications GmbH & Co. Verlag KG
(Singapore branch)
7030 Ang Mo Kio Ave 5
08-65 Northstar @ AMK, Singapore 569880
E-mail: apasin@singnet.com.sg

UK and Ireland
Dorling Kindersley Ltd
(a Penguin Company)
80 Strand, London, WC2R 0RL, UK
E-mail: sales@uk.dk.com

United States
Ingram Publisher Services
One Ingram Blvd, PO Box 3006
La Vergne, TN 37086-1986
E-mail: customer.service@ingrampublisher
services.com

Australia
Universal Publishers
PO Box 307
St. Leonards, NSW 1590
E-mail: sales@universalpublishers.com.au

INDEX

Tours

Palma

0   100

0   100